Rod-Building Guide

Fly • Spinning • Casting • Trolling

Tom Kirkman

Frank Amato

PORTLAND

Acknowledgments

In the twenty-some years during which I have been involved in the rod-building hobby/business, I have been extremely fortunate to come into contact with other rod builders, blank designers, epoxy formulators and tool makers, all of whom have helped shape my own knowledge of this craft. To claim all of the ideas in this book as springing from my own mind would be neither fair nor accurate. As such, I want to acknowledge the following individuals whose ideas and knowledge have contributed greatly to the information in this book.

I first met Ralph O'Quinn when I began publishing *RodMaker* Magazine. Ralph was the originator of the U-40 line of rod-building adhesives and finishes. His unique insight into this important part of the craft and his willingness to share with me has dispelled many myths that might otherwise have found their way into this book. Ralph's vast knowledge in this particular field enhanced that which I already knew and allowed me to add several important techniques to the chapter on finishing. Thanks to Ralph, I was able to address and hopefully eliminate many of the finishing problems that befall and bewitch so many rod builders.

Early in my own rod-building career, I had the good fortune to begin a long-term correspondence with a fellow named Gary Loomis. Gary was just starting his own blank-making company and yet even then I could understand the impact of what he would one day achieve. Our mutual correspondence, conversations and idea exchanges taught me much about the importance of materials, designs and construction of rod blanks. To this day I believe he has had a greater impact on advancements in blank-making technology than any other single individual. Thanks to Gary, I learned how weight reduction translates into better rod performance and this concept is heavily championed throughout the book. I believe it will help you to build a better rod.

The vast majority of what I know about rod building came about from making mistakes, and discussing these mistakes with other builders who were having similar difficulties. Often, a brainstorming session with other builders was enough to figure out where we had gone wrong and how to arrive at a workable solution. With that in mind, I want to thank Buddy Owens and Mike Bolt with whom I have shared and exchanged so many rod-building ideas. Very often, three heads proved far better than one.

Finally, thanks to my mom and dad, Janet and Thomas Kirkman, for all the time they spent indulging my fishing and rod-building habits over the years. For many years until I opened a permanent shop elsewhere, their basement was occupied by a horrendous array of fishing tackle and rod-building equipment. Also thanks to Wayne McGinnis on whose boat and fishing trips I was able to try so many new ideas on rods I had built. He was and still is a lousy guide, but he works cheap.

Published in 2001 by Frank Amato Publications, Inc.
P.O. Box 82112, Portland, Oregon 97282
(503) 653-8108 www.amatobooks.com

Softbound ISBN 10: 1-57188-216-2
Softbound ISBN 13: 978-1-57188-216-5
Softbound UPC: 0-66066-00430-7

All photographs taken by the author unless otherwise noted.
Book Design & Layout: Tony Amato

Printed in Singapore

10 9 8 7 6 5 4

Contents

Introduction

Many years ago, when the very first graphite rods made their appearance, I ordered one. It arrived damaged, and without knowledge of a local repairman, I was forced to make the necessary repairs myself. During the de-construction of that rod, I was appalled at what I thought was some pretty shoddy construction. I decided then and there that the next rod I owned would be one I had built myself. The next winter I embarked on that very endeavor, armed only with a bit of common sense, a mail-order catalog, and some very basic information. That first home-made custom rod proved to be the best-performing fishing rod I had ever used. On my first attempt I had created something that was not only up to the task but was extremely fun to fish with. I believe you can duplicate, or even better, those results as you build your first, or next, rod.

For many of you, building a rod will be a way to pass long, cold winter evenings. For others, it is a way to express your creativity with an item that you can actually use or provide for someone else's use. Some will undertake rod building in an effort to save a few bucks, while others will actually spend more than they would on a commercially-built rod in the hopes of having the very best rod that can be obtained. Whatever the reason, rod building is definitely fun, rewarding and more importantly, a craft at which anyone with decent manual dexterity, some patience and a bit of background information can excel. You don't need a room full of specialized tools nor a background in engineering in order to build a better rod than what you can find on the racks at your local tackle store. Most people who try their hand at rod building will ultimately build a second, then a third. For many, once the rod-building bug bites, it's hard to kick the habit. But getting started is the hard part for most people, many are afraid to push off into the unknown without someone or something to guide them. That's where I hope I can help.

When the publisher first contacted me about doing this book, we discussed just how involved and in-depth we wanted it to be. What we decided, was to try for a rod-building book that would fall in the middle of what is currently available. Something more than a simplistic beginner's book, but one that a beginner could understand and from which an old pro might glean some new techniques. With that in mind, forgive me if I do not go into tremendous detail on every facet of rod building, or if I seem to cover some topics with only the lightest touch. This time out, I am attempting to provide a general guide for the average person who is interested in building that very first rod or improving their next one. We'll leave the really heavy, technical stuff for a possible second book.

There is one last thought I want to impress upon you before we begin building a rod. Many people are very good at following instructions, but if they lose their place or fail to understand a particular instruction, they become lost and are unable to proceed without further instructions. If you are one of those people, and perhaps come to a point in this book where you suddenly find yourself scratching your head, all is not lost. Most of what is done in custom rod building follows the path of good sense. If you get lost, step back, assess the situation and use your own thoughts to figure out what seems to make the most sense. Sometimes simple reasoning can get you back on the road and moving again. Should that fail and as rod-building techniques, tools and topics continue to change, I want to make myself available to those of you who have this book and wish to discuss or find answers to current problems. I can be reached at rodmaker@earthlink.net and will attempt to provide answers, as time permits, on an individual basis. Now let's get started.

Blanks and Components

I have purposely left out any in-depth discussion of how blanks are made, as this is an area which few rod-builders will ever become directly involved in. However, in order to select the best possible blank for any specific rod-building endeavor, it is important for rod-builders to have a basic understanding of things like modulus, strain-rate, action and power and how they relate to blank properties. Understanding what these terms mean within the realm of rod building will help you to make the best possible choice when selecting a blank.

Modulus, Action and Power

The term you'll hear most often is "modulus". Simply put, this refers to how stiff a fiber is; how much it resists bending. As I write this, there are blanks which utilize fibers possessing a modulus of over 70 million psi! That's quite a number, but what does it really tell you about a rod blank? Well, it should be understood that the lighter a blank is for any given stiffness, the more efficient it can be in terms of accepting and releasing energy. It will translate more of the introduced energy into casting power and it will dampen (recover) more quickly than blanks which have the same stiffness, but are heavier.

The very best explanation on this subject I have ever heard came from Gary Loomis, founder of G. Loomis Inc. Gary liked to use the analogy of a diving board to illustrate the importance of stiffness-to-weight ratio. Let's say you jump on a diving board. It will throw you a certain distance into the air and then vibrate (oscillate) for a certain time afterwards before coming to a stop. Now if you take a fifty-pound sack of cement and tie it to the bottom of the same diving board, and then jump on it again, it won't throw you as high and will vibrate for a longer period of time before

Rod blanks are available in a multitude of lengths, powers and tapers. Sometimes the selection of models and materials can seem overwhelming. Your supplier is a good place to look for help in selecting the model that will best suit your needs.

coming to a stop. You didn't change its stiffness when you added that fifty-pound sack of cement, but you did increase the weight for the same amount of stiffness. That extra weight, for the same stiffness, resulted in a diving board that was less efficient. So modulus is indeed very important in terms of making a rod more efficient, but it does not tell the entire story.

The first rods made from graphite offered a tremendous reduction in weight. They possessed more stiffness for the amount of weight involved than any type of fiberglass and thus were able to offer better casting, better dampening and reduced fatigue on the fishermen. They were more efficient fishing tools, but they had a lower strain rate than fiberglass, thus they were not as tough. They broke far more easily than fiberglass rods from the same era. For many early graphite rod designers, the headache was in working with fibers that had a high modulus but a low strain rate (tensile strength). In fact, in those early days of graphite, as the modulus went up, the strain rate usually came down.

A few years later a fiber known as IM6 graphite came along. In addition to having a higher modulus than previous fibers, it also had a higher strain rate! Now it was possible to produce a rod that not only offered more stiffness for the weight, but more toughness as well. After IM6 came other fibers with even higher moduli and strain rates. Some people refer to this period as the "modulus wars" when companies would climb the modulus ladder in order to produce a lighter, perhaps better, rod or blank, only to be quickly bested by another firm using an even higher-modulus fiber. At any rate, this period produced some truly powerful, lightweight, strong rod blanks, but not without some misunderstandings on the part of rod builders.

Making a blank lighter is important in order to achieve better performance, but simply making it lighter alone is no guarantee that it is a better blank. Blank designers must balance a combination of properties in order to provide a product that will offer good fishability. The lightest blank in the world is worthless if it cannot withstand the normal abuse encountered in average fishing situations. Likewise, an unbreakable blank that is so heavy no one can stand to use it, really isn't going to be much fun to fish with. So what most blank designers shoot for is the lightest possible blank that still offers adequate durability. It is at this point that you must decide what qualities you most desire in a blank. If the utmost performance and efficiency is your goal, then a very high-modulus blank may be what you're after. Of course, such a blank will require more careful handling than one made from a lower-modulus fiber. (High-modulus rods are not "brittle" but they do require less material in order to achieve the same stiffness so there is less material involved and therefore a bit less durability.) If you desire a blank that will withstand rough handling, you would be advised to skip down the modulus scale and locate a blank that offers a bit more toughness, but with the knowledge that you are sacrificing some amount of performance in order to get that added durability.

Finally, I want to add that the blank which may be best from a pure efficiency standpoint, may not be the best in terms of what a particular fisherman may enjoy fishing with. The combination of power, action and construction material all contribute to a certain feel whose story cannot be told by modulus alone. Some fishermen will fish nothing but the highest-modulus, lightest rods out there. Others prefer rods made from lower-modulus fibers, and are just as productive on the lake or stream as anyone else. Part of the task of building a truly excellent custom rod is in selecting the particular blank that will perform best under the given circumstances for a particular fisherman. Simply buying the most expensive or the highest-modulus blank is no guarantee that you'll have the best rod. Take it from me, lower-modulus graphites, fiberglass and even bamboo are far from obsolete in many instances.

While the modulus wars were going on, many rod builders began banking on whatever blanks offered the highest modulus or the least weight for the needed stiffness. In so doing, many began to overlook the actual action (taper) and power of the blank. You cannot afford to do this. In fact, I suggest selecting your blank by first choosing the particular power and action that are needed for its desired purpose. The material or modulus of the fiber that the blank is made from should be the secondary consideration. The term "action" refers to the taper or where a blank bends when pressure is applied to it. Fast-action blanks will bend mostly in the upper 1/4 to 1/3 of their length while medium or moderate-action blanks can be expected to show most of their bending in the top half of the length. Slow-action blanks typically will bend over their entire length. Make no mistake, this is not to say that a fast-action rod will not bend down into the bottom half of its length if enough pressure is applied to it, just that the bending characteristics of the blank under nominal pressure, such as casting or working a lure or bait, will be as stated above. The action of any blank has much to do with how it will cast and how it will fight a fish.

The term "power" is pretty self explanatory. The greater the power listing the greater the amount of power the blank has for casting and fish fighting. When you look through a blank catalog you may find the power rating listed but more often you can get a good idea of what the actual power is by looking at the recommended casting and line weights. The higher these numbers are, the more powerful the blank will be. Matching these numbers to the lure weight you need to cast, and the line weight you intend to use, will eliminate most of the myriad of blanks available and trim down the selection process to a more manageable one.

Finally there is the age-old question of who makes the best blanks. Truthfully, most of the well-known blank makers are about on an even plane in terms of performance and quality. While it may be that one or the other has slightly higher-modulus graphite or a technique for making a slightly more durable blank, by and large the differences are minimal. To the best of my knowledge, among American blank makers there are no "bad" blanks. I suggest choosing your blank by finding the one that would appear to best fit your needs. If it happens to be made by company A, fine. If it happens to be made by company B, that's fine too. After you gain more experience in selecting and using blanks you will no doubt settle on just a few manufacturers as being your favorites. And do not choose a blank by price alone. While there are excellent blanks costing hundreds of dollars, some very, very good blanks are available for just a fraction of that amount.

Grips, Handles and Seats

Perhaps one of the greatest advantages of building your own rod is the chance to design and make the exact grip/reel-seat combination that best suits you and your particular type of fishing. In the photo, you will see the most common grip and seat combinations for most fishing applications. There is no reason why you cannot deviate from any of these if you have a special requirement that standard set-ups do not fill. At the very least, you will want to decide upon lengths and diameters that will fit your personal requirements.

There really is no wrong way to build a handle, but there are some mistakes common to novice rod builders that should be discussed. The length of the butt grip on any rod is critical to ensure the usefulness and comfort of the rod. Do you require a long grip for two-handed casting? Will you be inserting your rod into some type of holder that precludes a large-diameter grip? These are the type of questions you must ask yourself before deciding upon lengths and diameters. For most light to medium freshwater fishing, butt grips are kept short because the casting and fish fighting is centered around the reel seat. On heavier freshwater, and most saltwater rods, a longer butt grip is helpful as it allows the angler to exert more leverage on the fish by placing the rod butt under the forearm or elbow, thereby sparing the wrist from unnecessary strain. A bit of testing and thinking will allow you to arrive at the most beneficial length before construction begins.

Foregrips are equally important. On lighter spinning rods, the foregrip rarely comes into play, as the fish-fighting hand is usually directly on the reel seat. On heavier rods, both casting and spinning types, fighting a large fish may require that a hand be placed on a sufficiently long foregrip. On some offshore rods, particularly those rods known as stand-up rods where the angler uses leverage and body strength to fight large fish, the foregrip may be longer than the butt grip!

Fortunately, even first-time builders usually have some rods lying around that can be used as a reference or starting

Reel seats, grips and end caps are available in various styles and sizes.
Your choice will be determined by the type of rod you are building as well as your particular taste.

point. Pick out your favorite rod, one that is at least similar in type and size to what you plan to build. Ask yourself what you like and don't like about the grip lengths and diameters on that rod. Write down your preferred lengths on your planning sheet for butt and fore grips. Remember, you can make them any length you prefer.

After you have determined what you think you would like as far as grip lengths, you must do some testing. Make some temporary masking tape bushings and locate where your reel seat would be if you used the grip lengths you have written down. Go outside and work through some casting motions. Better yet, tape on some guides (more on this coming up) and do some actual casting. Have someone hold the end of your line and "fight" them as if you were working against a fish. Such testing will soon tell you if the lengths you have decided on will be comfortable and effective for you. It is likely that you will have to adjust the lengths of your grips. No problem, shift the seat to allow for any adjustments and continue testing. Once you have arrived at the optimum grip lengths, enter these on your planning sheet.

Now you are faced with deciding what grip material to use. Cork is the all-time favorite, and with good reason. It's light, rigid and holds up very well in the elements. Of course, there are various grades of cork, with some of the poorer grades having a good many pits and holes dotting the surface. Does this necessarily hurt anything? Yes and no. Really bad cork can be uncomfortable to hold, particularly on a fly rod where your hand stays on the grip all the time. But in many instances, cork imperfections are just a cosmetic issue. If you desire a really, really nice cork grip, you may have to abandon preformed cork grips and make your own from individual rings (more on that coming up). Most preformed cork grips are made from average, at best, cork rings and then the imperfections are filled with some type of paste in order to improve the appearance. Unfortunately, this filler usually falls out after a bit of use, leaving the original imperfections on display. But again, surface imperfections are, for the most part, a cosmetic issue and have little bearing on rod performance.

What about synthetic foam grips? In many instances, these can be as good or better than cork. Again, grades vary although what we are dealing with now is not surface imperfections, but type and hardness. Most foam grips have a hardness rating of about 40 to 60 durometers (figure 100 durometers being absolutely firm, like cork). I can tell you that the softer and more spongy the grip is, the less you will like it over time. Personally, I have always favored synthetic foam grips with a hardness rating of at least 65 durometers or higher, feeling that it handles better and lasts longer. Trouble is, foam grips of that hardness are difficult to find. If you live near a shop that sells rod components, by all means go in and look—and feel—what they have. Never be afraid to order different types, and arrange with the dealer to return any that do not suit you. Look for a grip that is reasonably firm, yet still relatively light in weight. Stick your thumbnail deep into it and see how long it takes to recover. All foam grips will "bruise" to some extent, but such bruising should resolve itself within minutes. If it doesn't, you are looking at a grip that has a great deal of memory and will show every pressure point put upon it, for the life of the rod.

I know that for some of you, deciding on the type, style and length of grips may be a daunting task. In that instance, you may wish to take a look at some of the grip and handle kits that some dealers offer. While such kits tend to "lock you in" to specific lengths and diameters, there are some good kits on the market and if you spot one that is very close to what your planning sheet calls for, you can save some time by choosing one. Keep in mind that the grips sold in kits can also be modified as to length and diameter if need be.

Guides

Today's rod builder can choose from a larger selection of guides than at any time in the history of rod building. Not only has the selection of frame sizes and styles mushroomed, but the inserts within those guides are now offered in a truly huge number of materials. For the beginner, the selection of guides can be bewildering if not downright confusing. But it needn't be that hard.

Frame Types

The basic task of a line guide is to control the line during casting and fish fighting. As you read further into this book, you will notice that I constantly speak of selecting and using the lightest components that will do the necessary job. This advice is sound for guide selection as well.

The frame type you choose should be the lightest that will still provide adequate durability for what the rod is expected to encounter. Obviously, a heavy-duty boat rod will require guides made with stronger frames than a rod meant for ultra-light spin fishing. There is no need to over-gun when selecting guide frame style. Choose the lightest style that will hold up and do the job for the particular type of fishing you will be doing.

As you read the chapter on guide spacing you begin to develop a feel for the height you need in the guides for any particular rod. This is one area where rod builders have a vastly better selection from which to choose. But be careful not to buy into the idea that certain type guides can only be used on certain types of rods. For instance, most low-framed guides are generally considered to be casting guides, while higher-frame guides are usually specified as being for spinning rods. Depending on what you need to achieve, you may find that a higher-framed guide works great on a particular casting rod, or that lower-framed guides really perform on the tip section of your spinning rod. If you have no experience in selecting and buying from the various guides available, I suggest you first read the chapter on guide placement so that you will have some good background information as to what type and style guide will best suit your needs.

Again, your selection will depend upon the type of rod you are building.
This is a small sample of the various types and styles of guides available to the rod builder.

Ring Materials

For many years most guides where made from a single material. With the exception of steel guides carrying agate or ruby rings, most guides were simple steel frames with steel rings. Sometimes a hard chrome plating was applied to the ring to make it more durable and resistant to wear. In the mid to late 1960s new guides with ceramic rings were introduced. They were an instant hit, as they did not groove from the action of the line moving back and forth across the surface. This made guide replacement due to normal wear almost unheard of. But these early ceramic-ringed guides were also heavy and sometimes spit out their rings after a hard knock or two! Luckily, the guides you have to choose from today are much, much better in this regard. Newer, lighter, smoother types of ceramic rings are often fastened directly into the guide frames and provide excellent durability along with stunning performance.

Today, there are two main guide ring materials; ceramic and metal matrix, although there are many types within those two subgroups. So how do you choose? For many builders, money will be a consideration. The better, lighter, slicker rings are fairly expensive when you consider that some awfully good rings are available at very little expense. In fact, once you move past a particular price point, much of

what you will be paying for will go unnoticed in terms of actual fishing performance. With that said, I am going to steer you away from the old-fashioned stainless steel or hard chromed rings (which are still available and favored by some diehards) and suggest the best ceramic or metal matrix rings you can afford.

For most general-purpose rods, a good aluminum oxide guide ring is more than sufficient. In fact, not too many years ago, guide rings made from aluminum oxide were the absolute top of the line! Over the past few years they have been refined even further and inset into frames that are lighter yet stronger than ever. There are various grades of aluminum oxide and depending upon the particular guide manufacturer they are marketed under various names. Most of them will stand up for many, many years under the wear of monofilament line and may actually outlast the rest of the rod. Selecting a high-quality aluminum oxide guide is usually a safe bet.

As new guide ring materials continue to be developed, it is likely that I am going to bypass some of them for what many anglers consider to be the best guide ring material available today—silicon carbide. But if you want to move up to the next level of performance, I strongly suggest silicon carbide rings. Harder and able to be polished to a much slicker surface, silicon carbide offers truly outstanding resistance to grooving and cutting, even from the new generation of Kevlar/plastic fishing lines which have proven quite harsh on sub-standard guide rings. But they won't cut a good silicon carbide ring. In fact, you can quickly dull a good file on a silicon carbide ring without any damage to the ring itself! Rings made from silicon carbide also dissipate heat fairly quickly, making them a good choice for both heavy saltwater applications where a fish makes hard charging, smoking runs, dragging the line out under great pressure against the guide rings, as well as for the light-line angler who needs to protect fine-diameter lines during long fights. Different manufacturers will sell rings made from silicon carbide under various names, but will usually explain that they are in fact, silicon carbide. Most of those of which I am aware are very good and if you are willing to spend just a tad more money for the silicon carbine, you will be rewarded with a guide whose slickness can literally be felt during casting and retrieving.

Over and above the ceramics are what many people refer to as metal matrix guides. The most notable of these at this writing are Fuji's Cermet guide rings, although other companies will surely introduce their own versions by the time you read this. Even harder and slicker than silicon carbide, Cermet rings are also crafted a bit lighter and thinner, reducing weight and increasing performance. But here is where we get into an area of diminishing returns. While I have no doubt that these are the hardest, lightest, slickest guide rings yet produced, the question of just how much better of a performance they offer against the tremendous increase in cost must be asked. Most fishermen, being only human, are unable to detect any noticeable difference between the better silicon carbide guides and the best metal matrix rings. While it is true that tests have been performed which prove the metal matrix rings to be superior on every front, you must still decide if a 10 percent increase in performance justifies a 100 percent increase in cost, particularly when silicon carbide guides are so good to begin with. But if you want the best, and don't mind paying for it, then a Cermet guide rings set in titanium frames should make you happy. But it will set you back a sizable sum of money.

Without sufficient rod-building experience, many of you reading this will still have a hard time deciding upon what type guides to buy for your rod-building project. Again I recommend either a high-quality aluminum oxide or silicon carbide ring in either a steel or titanium frame. Beyond that, I strongly suggest asking your blank and component dealer for his or her recommendations. After a while, you will begin to favor particular guide styles for particular rods.

Fly and Trolling Guides

These two rod types have traditionally called for slightly different types of guides than those used on all other rod types. In the case of fly rods, there are now high-quality ceramic-ringed guides which pretty much make the old wire/steel snake guides obsolete on every front. I know some people will gasp when they read such a statement, preferring to believe that snake guides possess some sort of special magic that enables them to remain the optimum fly-rod guide for all eternity. Unfortunately, that just isn't the case. Just as they superseded the old ring-and-clasp guide, so modern ceramic guides have relegated the snake guide to the antique shelf. Still, this statement will remain upsetting to many fly fishermen who feel that if nothing else, the snake guide must be held onto for tradition's sake. Considering that they are being wrapped onto non-traditional graphite blanks and fish with equally non-traditional plastic fly lines, I suggest dropping the "tradition" argument and moving ahead into a new realm of rod performance. Properly selected and utilized ceramic fly-rod guides will outperform and outlast the best snake guides. Continue to argue if you must, but by all means try some modern guides with an open mind and be prepared for a surprise.

Heavy IGFA offshore trolling and stand-up rods require something a bit different in guide design. Earlier I spoke of the heat generated when fishing line is pulled, under pressure and at great speed, across the surface of a line guide. This heat will quickly destroy line and thus special guides with rolling line guide wheels were developed. Commonly referred to as "roller guides" these are still the best choice for any heavy, powerful rods destined to fight truly large and strong fish. Because the line guide rolls, thereby moving with the line instead of the line sliding across the guide surface, heat is reduced if not totally eliminated. Obviously, such guides require keen maintenance, otherwise they can lock up and you are back to the line dragging across a stationary surface.

There are some silicon carbon and silicon nitride guides which are marketed as suitable alternatives to roller guides. To a great extent, they are an excellent guide for even heavy trolling rods. They dissipate heat well enough that line failure from such is not much of an issue. I have personally used them on rods up to IGFA 80-pound class and have seen them perform perfectly and without incident over the course of more than a decade of hard use. So which is better, roller or silicon carbide? On rods of 50-pound and under, I believe that they are both equally good. The rollers require a bit more in terms of maintenance, the silicon carbides, in such large sizes, are a bit more expensive. For most people the choice will come down to one of personal preference. For myself, I now use the silicon carbide almost exclusively on all stand-up and trolling rods from up to 50-pound class. For rods used with 80-pound and above line, I have stayed with rollers.

Guide Sets

I have never been particularly excited by the guide sets offered by many of the rod-building vendors. If you don't have a clue as to what to select, or just don't want to spend the time learning, then picking a set based on a catalog's listing will suffice, but may not offer the highest level of performance. Many of my best-performing rods have a combination of "casting" and "spinning" guides on the same rod. As you progress further into the craft, you should begin to recognize which guides will perform best in certain situations and select accordingly. Until then, chew on the information presented here and always consider discussing your choice with your blank and component supplier.

Wrapping Thread

While it's true that you could just use any old type of thread, specialty rod-winding thread offers greater ease of use, better final appearance and lasts far longer than anything else you could use. There are a handful of companies that make these specialty threads, and your blank and component supplier will carry a full range of colors and sizes from at least one of them. Thread is extremely inexpensive. A single 100-yard spool is usually more than enough for wrapping an entire rod, even allowing for you to remove and rewrap any guides that are not to your satisfaction. Many rod builders will go ahead and stock up on a few spools of different sizes and colors so that they will be readily available should any colorful inspiration suddenly strike.

For the most part, only two sizes are now used in rod building, size A and size D. Size A is the smaller in diameter of the two and is generally used for all fly rods and on ultra-light through heavy freshwater rods. Larger saltwater rods may sometimes benefit from the use of the larger-diameter D thread, but maybe not for the reasons you would suspect. The holding power of a thread is derived more from the number of thread winds per inch, and not from diameter. And since great tension is not required, as you will understand in a minute, large-diameter threads do not offer any advantages in guide-holding power and are actually a bit harder to finish nicely. For these reasons, size A thread is generally used on all rods except those where greater resistance to hard wear and tear is required. Heavy-power surf, boat and trolling rods, or any rod where abrasion and rough handling is expected should be wrapped with D thread, while all others will be served nicely with A. Size A is a bit harder to see and work with owing to its smaller diameter, so many beginners are tempted to use D.

Still, unless you are not able to see well, and cannot rectify that with glasses or magnification of some sort, you will be better off using A thread on any rods outside of the heavier, sometimes rough service rods as those mentioned previously.

You are still faced with choosing between two basic rod-winding thread types; Regular Nylon and NCP. Regular Nylon is a beautiful thread with subtle sparkle in the sunlight, but must be coated with a color preserver sealer prior to finishing in order to retain its original color or it will darken from its original shade and in some cases turn almost transparent. NCP is an opaque thread designed to be used and finished without the application of color preserver as it will retain its original color either way. However, NCP is a dull, paint like color thread that does little to enhance the appearance of a nice custom rod. Many rod builders use it with good results, and perhaps even like the way it looks. My personal use of NCP, however, is limited to the occasional use of it for small trim wraps or on some decorative butt wraps where I wish to keep color bleed-through to a minimum. The majority of rod builders will agree that Regular Nylon thread looks better, winds more smoothly and lasts longer than NCP.

With that said, I want to finish this chapter by giving you a bit of advice on the best place to purchase your rod-building blanks, components and supplies. If you simply shop around for the best price you will be doing yourself a great disservice. It will be to your advantage to buy from the dealer or dealers who offer you the best service and advice. Oftentimes, an extra measure of service or helpful advice is truly invaluable and this is why I believe most rod builders are better off buying from specialty blank and component dealers. The people who own and staff such establishments are rod builders themselves. They understand the rod-building process and most are eager to help you in any way they can. Rarely are they any more expensive than the mass merchandisers, but even if you end up spending a couple bucks more when buying from them, the service they offer when you someday find yourself in a bind or with a question will more than make up the difference. Please trust me on this.

Chapter 2

Tools

Tools

For the most part, rod building does not require any specialized tooling. There are, however, a few simple tools that you can make yourself which will make your rod-building tasks easier and more productive.

Tapered Reamers

Sometimes even very simple tools can be the most useful. Tapered reamers are not only useful but very easy and inexpensive to make as well.

    While you can use an ordinary round file for enlarging the inside diameter of cork and EVA grips, a properly made tapered reamer will remove material much faster. Having several sizes on hand permits accurate centering of the hole in the grip or handle.

    The accompanying photos show how to make a tapered reamer from start to finish. All you need to begin is a scrap piece from an old rod, preferably with a heavy wall, some slow-cure epoxy adhesive and some cutting grit. (Cutting grit is available from various rod-building houses.)

    If you make several reamers, each from a different diameter or tapered section of old rod, you can always arrive at just the right reamer size for a particular job. Reamers work best when they are only slightly smaller than the hole you wish to enlarge. As soon as the hole begins to enlarge, switch to the next largest reamer size and you will find it much easier to keep the hole centered in the grip. For years I have kept as many as a dozen reamers on hand for performing grip I.D. enlargement and having such a selection of

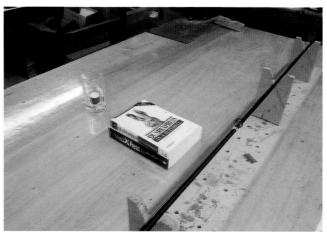

Here is a simple wrapping set-up. A set of V-blocks mounted to a base supports the blank while a glass mug or coffee cup holds a spool of thread. The thread is run up out of the cup and through a book which provides tension for the wrap. Adding more books, or removing some, allows you to effectively adjust thread tension.

sizes makes it easy to pick the right tool for the job. Reamers are easy to make, and very inexpensive, so it makes good sense to put several together at a time.

    Please note that reamers such as these are intended for hand use only. Do not use them in any type of drill or lathe as the heat from friction can break down the epoxy bond and release cutting grit at very high speeds.

Rod Wrappers/Lathes

There are many specialty rod wrappers and rod-building lathes on the market today. Some are very basic units consisting of a wooden base and simple uprights for holding a rod blank, while others are precision machines which allow you to not only wrap a rod, but turn and shape grips, bore hosels and arbors, and accomplish a host of other tasks as well. I would discourage a beginning rod builder from buying anything other than the most simple wrapping set-up for the time being. As you progress, you will get a better idea of the type of rods you will be building and the exact tasks you will need to perform on those rods. At that time you will have a better idea of what type of wrapper or lathe would best suit the work you are doing and can then make a wise decision and practical investment in a unit that will serve you for years to come. In the meantime, you can get by just fine with a simple set of "V" blocks and a wooden base, coupled with some books for thread tension and a coffee mug to hold the spool. Early in my own rod-building career, I used such a set-up to wrap dozens of rods. The quality of those rods was just as good as any of the rods made on my

A set of simple V-blocks, independent or affixed to a base, will suffice for the first-time rod builder. In the forefront of this photo, notice the commercially made wrap tensioner. Such devices, as well as complete wrapping jigs and lathes, are available for those who wish. They are not necessary, but nice if you plan to build many rods.

$1000 specialty rod lathes. It just took a tad longer, that's all. If you have access to some simple tools you can make your own set of "V" blocks. Failing that, simple rod-wrapping units are available ready-made for under $60. If you plan on wrapping more than one rod and don't want the bother of making your own, they are a good investment.

If you have made enough rods to have some idea of what features you would like in a lathe or wrapper, then I suggest sending for the various catalogs and brochures of the wrapper/lathe manufacturers. Ask your current blank and component distributor what brand or brands he or she carries and the features of each. Don't rush into buying the first one that you see. Take your time and thoroughly investigate each unit until you find one that offers the features you need for the type of work you do most often.

Miscellaneous

Before you begin building your rod, you'll want to gather up a few sheets of sandpaper in medium and fine grades. Some isopropyl or solvent alcohol and a roll of paper towels will be needed for cleaning parts and general clean-up. Get yourself some single-edge razor blades for trimming wrapping threads and an inexpensive ox hair brush, preferably flat and soft, for applying finish.

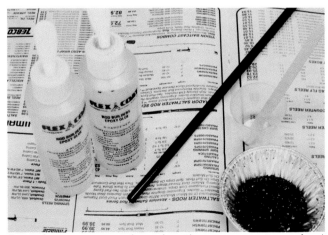

These tapered reamers were made by gluing cutting grip to scrap pieces of blank with epoxy. You can make them yourself, or purchase them from any rod-building supply house. They are helpful for enlarging cork and EVA grip inside diameters. Along with some sandpaper, a few files and a razor blade for cutting thread, your rod-building tool kit is basically complete.

Step 1: Apply the epoxy liberally to the piece of rod blank and allow it to sit for a few minutes.

Tapered reamers are easily made with some scrap pieces of rod blank, cutting grit and 2-part slow-cure epoxy (Do not attempt to use the 5-minute variety).

Step 2: Sprinkle the cutting grit over and around the epoxy-coated blank. Set the blank aside to dry. Gather up the newspaper and pour any loose cutting grit back into the original container for use on future reamers.

Now would be a good time to discuss the adhesives and glues used in bonding grips, handles and reel seats. Some very bad information on adhesives continues to travel in rod-building circles and has contributed to both catastrophic failures and minor, yet very annoying, movement of handle and grip assemblies.

Contrary to popular belief, the strongest adhesive in the world will do little good if it is used in the wrong manner or the wrong situation. Too many rod builders believe that if a little adhesive is good, then a lot is better! They pour gobs of adhesive down into handle and seat joints, mistakenly thinking that they are making these assemblies stronger. In reality, they are only making them heavier, not stronger. Before we can properly assemble our grips and handles and seats, we need a bit of background on proper rod-building adhesives. How they work, when to use which one, and how to apply each.

Rod-Building Adhesives

For all intents and purposes, you can get by with just one or two adhesives for the vast majority of rod-building chores. The adhesive you hear about most when it comes to rod-building is two-part epoxy. While there are many different types and brands of two-part epoxies, there are only three or four that serve a purpose as far as rod building is concerned. The first is the quick-set "5-minute" variety. Normally, use of such a quick-setting epoxy is limited to the installation of tip-tops. It works well for this particular rod building task as it forms a secure connection on any type rod-between tip-top and rod blank and yet its bond can still be broken with a brief application of heat from a butane lighter or match. This allows damaged tip-tops to be easily replaced. Due to its truly fast setting property, however, it is unwise to use it for the assembly of grips or reel seats. If you attempt to use it for these other chores, I can promise you that at some point it will "set" before you get things lined up and a minor rod-building catastrophe will have occurred. Limit its use to mounting tip-tops and tip-tops only.

Slow-curing epoxy, such as those marketed by most of the same companies who make rod-building epoxy thread-wrap finishes, is the most widely used epoxy for rod-building tasks. Typical epoxies in this genre will set in about 30 minutes to an hour and cure enough for any bond to be stressed in just a few hours. This type of epoxy is usually of a thin consistency (low viscosity). This makes it ideal for snug-fitting joints such as grip and handle assemblies where thicker epoxies would simply be pushed out of the joint.

Devcon, Epoxy Coatings Company, Flex Coat and Trondak U-40 all make excellent slow-cure two-part epoxies.

The folks at Trondak, home of the U-40 rod-building product line, also make a specialty rod-building epoxy called Rod Bond. It has been compounded specifically for rod-building tasks. Having a consistency about the same as Vaseline helps keep it in the joint rather than seeping or running out as some thinner epoxies do. It also remains fairly flexible which makes it ideal on fishing rods which are subject to flex, expansion, contraction and sometimes a bit of rough handling. Although I still prefer the regular two-part epoxies mentioned above for mounting synthetic grips, Rod Bond is making tremendous inroads among rod builders as the adhesive of choice for a myriad of rod-building chores. Because it is more of a gel, rather than a runny liquid, it requires a tad bit more space between components in order to remain in the joint.

Gap-filling epoxies, PC-7 being perhaps the best example, serve to take up space in joints where a loose fit or void requires an adhesive with gap-filling properties. These epoxies are heavy, thick, viscous adhesives that retain strength when used liberally in joints with voids that must be filled. All too often, however, unthinking rod builders will use these thick epoxies in tight-fitting joints and the stuff just gets pushed out of the joint completely. Failure at that point usually occurs down the line and the epoxy is blamed when in reality the joint failed because someone used a good product in the wrong application. I no longer recommend its use in the area of rod building however, as anything it can do, either RodBond or a better-fitting joint can accomplish just as well, and with a lot less fuss.

Finally, there are the various types of "hot melt" glues. Actually, the use of such glue goes back a long way with the old Gudebrod Ferrule Cement which you heated and then dripped or smeared in the joint. Once cooled, it retained the pieces, yet could be heated later allowing for repair or replacement of damaged parts. Use of "hot melt" glue is now normally limited to the installation of tip-tops. For light rods, or those whose tips are frequently damaged and need constant replacement, it is a decent adhesive. But be warned, tip-tops mounted with even the high-temp hot melt glues are subject to twisting in hot climates and under hard use. Use it if you must, keep some on hand for emergency repairs, but limit it for use on lighter freshwater rods.

Joints

Even the strongest epoxies are no help when used in poor fitting or contaminated joints. Relying on any adhesive to salvage a truly sloppy fit, or to bond dirty, contaminated parts is ill advised. Copious amounts of adhesive DO NOT in any way make up for laziness or sloppiness on the part of the rod builder.

In order to get a strong joint, you must achieve a fit that allows for some epoxy to get, and stay, between the parts. This is accomplished by either creating a bit of space between the mating parts, or cutting channels on the surfaces of close-fitting parts. Either way, this allows the adhesive to get inside the joint and "lock" things in place. Epoxy has both cohesive and adhesive strength and can be used in a bit thicker line than some other glues and adhesives that lack cohesive strength. But don't get carried away—keep the fit between your parts close, but not tight, and you should be okay. The only exception will be on parts such as EVA and/or cork grips and rings where absorption of the epoxy will keep the adhesive in the joint. In these instances, it is okay and actually preferred to have a very snug-fitting assembly. More on that later.

Preparation

Surfaces of non-absorbent parts should be moderately scuffed with fine grit (400 grit) sandpaper or a Scotchbrite pad. It is not necessary to gouge or deeply scar the surfaces, but they should be thoroughly scuffed. This helps to provide a surface that the epoxy can wet and adhere to.

Once the parts have been properly fitted and prepped for assembly, they must be thoroughly cleaned. I suggest either denatured solvent alcohol or 90% isopropyl alcohol for this purpose. It is not necessary to use anything more volatile. Wipe all mating surfaces thoroughly with a rag wetted with alcohol and allow a minute or two for them to completely dry.

Two-part epoxies should be measured and mixed according to their respective directions. Most are designed to be used in a 1 to 1 system, that is 1 part resin to 1 part hardener. It is important to try and achieve a mix that is as close as possible to the recommended ratio. And don't think that by adding extra hardener you can get the stuff to set up more quickly. It might, but the adhesive properties of the epoxy may be compromised as well.

When applying the adhesive, pay attention to where you put it! With reel seat arbors, bushings, reel seats, etc., where you may be sliding one part over another, you do not want to push the adhesive out of the joint while doing so. You may need to apply it to both surfaces or perhaps higher up on the blank where it will come in contact with and coat all surfaces before the final fit is reached. The idea is to have the epoxy in, through and between the joint. Let me assure you that clean, properly fitted parts joined with the correct adhesive become one solid and secure unit forever.

Chapter 4

Understanding Rod Spine

If you're new to rod building, you may not be aware that fishing-rod blanks possess a property known as the *spine*. Even many long-time builders are confused by this property and have a hard time locating and utilizing the spine. Simply put, a rod blank's spine is that plane or axis where the blank exhibits its least resistance to bending. The spine is generally referred to, by most rod builders anyway, as the *outside* of curve when the blank is bent into a curve of least resistance. In other words, the outside of what rod builders call the *relaxed curve*.

How do you find it? It's pretty simple; just locate a smooth, flat, hard surface and we'll go to work. Notice in the photo below that we have the butt end of the blank on a hard, flat surface. One hand is pressuring the blank in the middle, enough to put a decent bend in it. The other hand is supporting the blank at the extreme tip in such a way that the blank is free to rotate until it comes to rest in a relaxed position. (Remember to support the blank at the extreme tip as we are seeking the effect of the spine over the entire length of the blank, not just a portion of it.) Allow the blank to roll until it naturally comes to rest in the position where it seems to want to return each time you attempt to roll it out of that position. This will be the *relaxed curve*. It is the *outside* of this curve that you should mark and refer to as the spine. Doing so will allow you to follow and understand the discussions of most other rod builders.

To find the effective spine on your blank, place the butt end on a hard, smooth surface and support the extreme tip end in one hand. Now press down in the center with your other hand and allow the blank to roll into a gentle bend of least resistance. You will know this when it occurs, as this is the position the blank will seem to want to remain in. You are not looking for a "kick" or a "jump" but rather are allowing the blank to come to rest in its own preferred bend. Mark the *outside* or underneath of this "relaxed curve" as the effective spine.

As I said earlier, a good deal of confusion still exists, even among those builders who have built many rods, over just what it is you are feeling for when trying to locate the spine. Some try to find the point where the blank jumps or kicks away, but what they are locating with such a method is not the spine. Likewise, supporting the blank between two chairs or uprights will cause the blank to roll to a stationary position, but this is the effect of the blank's natural curvature which may or may not be in line with the spine. What you want to find is that point of least resistance which the blank exhibits when it is pressured into a curve. When the blank stops fighting you, and comes to rest in a position where it seems to want to stay, you've found it. the outside of that curve, is the spine. Okay, now that you've located the spine, what do you do with it? Where should you put your guides? Let's delve into this thing a bit further and determine where you need to locate the spine for your particular fishing requirements.

First off, you must understand that when a rod blank is constructed, a pattern is cut from a prepeg (fiber and resin combined in a matrix) material and wound around a tapered mandrel. Try to picture what happens when what appears to the casual observer as a sort of haphazard triangle, is wound around a steel mandrel which is rather tiny at one end, and quite a bit larger at the other. Hopefully you can see that the wall thickness of the fiber around the circumference as well as along the entire length of the blank will vary. This uneven wall thickness around and along the blank results in varying stiffness or resistance to bending, along any given plane of the blank. At some point, on some plane, there will be a position where the resistance to bending will be the least. It is the *outside* of the curve formed when the blank is bent into a curve of least resistance or *relaxed curve* that most rod builders now refer to as the "spine".

So what if the blank does exhibit a plane of least resistance? Well, many builders have felt that this tendency for the blank to favor this particular plane when pressure is applied, means that the only way to have a stable rod, free from any tendency to twist under pressure, is to position the guides so that the finished rod is fished in exactly this position. That would be spine on top, plane of least resistance towards the fish. On a casting rod, the guides would be on top of the spine, and with fly or spinning rods the guides would be underneath, or 180-degrees opposite the spine. A rod built in this manner will certainly fish fine. But it won't necessarily be as stable as you might hope, particularly if you're building a casting rod with the guides located on top of the rod.

This tool is known as a spine finder. It consists of two ball bearings mounted in a wooden support. While it makes finding the effective spine quite easy, it is not an absolute necessity.

Using the spine finder you are also seeking the bend of least resistance or "relaxed curve". When the blank comes to rest, under pressure and does not seem to want to leave that position, mark the *outside* of the curve, in this case the top, as the effective spine.

Follow the sequence of pictures. In the first photo, a blank has been inserted into a spine finder (a special tool for locating the spine, but no more accurate than the simple hand method outlined earlier) and the tip has been pressured by hand. The blank has rolled into the bend of least resistance and the top, or the outside, of the bend will be marked as the spine. This position will henceforth be referred to as the relaxed curve, with the outside of the curve referred to as the spine. In the second photo, casting-rod guides have been taped on top of this relaxed curve and a line run through the guides and attached to a 1-pound weight. According to many builders, when the weight is released and the blank accepts the load, this positioning of the spine will prevent rod twist and the blank will remain stable.

Unfortunately, such is not the case. In the photos at the right the weight has been released and the blank has spun so the the spine is now directly on the bottom along with the guides. What happened? The simple fact is that the line, under pressure, sought the lowest point and spun the rod 180-degrees, overcoming the effect of the spine. Even if we

were to repeat this test, but this time put the spine on the bottom and the guides on top, directly 180 degrees opposite the spine, the rod would still twist or roll under pressure until the guides were on the bottom. Simply put, this shows that in some instances, guide positioning and location affect rod stability more than the spine does.

Obviously, had we performed the same test with fly or spinning guides taped to the bottom of the rod, spine once again on top, the rod would not have spun. But not so much because the spine was facing up, but rather because the guides were already positioned to allow the line to reach the lowest point automatically. If you reverse the procedure, putting your spinning or fly guides directly on the spine, rolling them to the bottom and applying pressure to the line, they will overcome the effect of the spine and remain on the bottom. Regardless of what you may have heard, they will not spin to the top.

So what does this prove? Just that the position of the spine has less to do with rod stability than the position of the guides do. With this demonstrated, you are freed from necessarily having to locate the guides in any particular position in relation to the spine in order to prevent rod twist. Rods where the guides are located on the bottom of the rod will not try to twist regardless of where they are located in relation to the spine. Likewise, on normal casting rods, line pressure will always try to twist the rod no matter where you locate the spine relative to the guides. If you're holding the rod, it may not spin in your hands, but the tip end will most likely exhibit some twist.

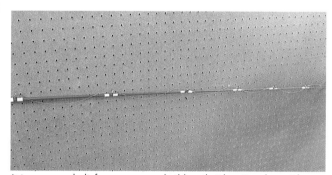

It is common belief among many builders that locating the guides on a casting rod on the effective spine will prevent rod twist under pressure. We have done just that in this photo.

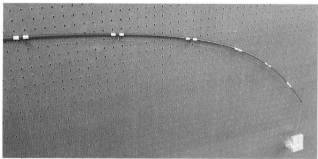

When pressure is applied however, in this case via a heavy weight, the guides rotate to the bottom as the line seeks the lowest point. While the spine is an important consideration in terms of overall rod performance, it cannot be utilized to make a rod stable under load as was once commonly believed.

What about torsional forces trying to tear the rod apart internally if you fail to locate the spine on top? While these forces certainly exist, they do not seem to be responsible for rod failures in any significant numbers. Any type of force generated by torsional twisting is applied to the resin holding the fibers together. Modern resin systems seem more than adequate in withstanding such forces.

But that's not the whole story either. A rod must do more than just fight a fish. In most cases it must cast a line or lure, and you want it to do that in such a manner that allows the most distance and accuracy. Now the spine comes back into play. In order to achieve the most distance and casting accuracy from either spinning, casting or fly rods, most rod builders agree that the guides need to be either on, or directly 180 degrees opposite, the spine. I suggest this test: locate the spine and position the spine on top and locate/tape the guides on top of the spine (doesn't matter whether it's a casting or other type rod, both positions will be tested). Now go do some test casting, making sure you are able to measure both distance and accuracy. Now remove the guides and tape them into position 180 degrees opposite the spine and try the same casting tests. You should notice quite a bit of difference between the two placements and can then easily determine where you should place your guides in order to achieve the best distance and accuracy for the particular type of rod you are building. Obviously, this particular position will be exactly opposite between casting and fly/spinning rods.

This is the point where some astute builders will mention that hardly anyone can cast on a perfect plane, managing to keep the spine exactly in line with the casting stroke. There's no point in arguing this point, as it is true. But that is no reason to fail to build the rod without regarding the spine. I feel that if there is going to be a limiting factor in a rod's performance, it should be the skill of the angler, not the design of the rod.

So the spine does make a difference, often a huge difference in terms of the castability of a rod. But not so much in terms of rod stability. Luckily, spinning and fly rods are going to be stable just by the very nature of the guides being on the bottom of the rod and allowing the line to seek the lowest point without having to twist or spin the rod. Not so with casting rods however, unless you utilize something known as a spiral or Roberts wrap, whereby the guides are gradually spun around the blank so that they end up on the bottom of the rod. By rotating the guides on a casting rod around the blank, so that they ultimately locate on the bottom of the rod, the rod no longer exhibits a tendency to twist and remains stable. This is the only method which I am aware of that allows for a truly stable casting rod regardless of where you choose to position the spine. More on this type of guide set-up can be found in Chapter 6 "Guide Placement."

There is one last option to consider however, and it seems to completely disregard the spine in terms of guide position. Still it offers for many builders the best rod in terms of overall fishing attributes. During your attempts to locate the spine, you have no doubt noticed that just as any blank has a plane of least resistance, it also has a plane of greatest resistance. This plane, sometimes referred to as the "hard side," may or may not be directly 180 degrees opposite the spine. Most times it won't be. In fact, more often it is located along the natural curvature of the blank. I suggest trying to locate it by hand or with a spine finder; locating the plane where the blank keeps trying to jump away, equally to one side or the other. It's sort of a balancing act, a bit tricky but it can be done. (I suppose we could call this the *distraught* curve!) In many cases you will find that this puts you bending directly *against* the normal concave bend of the blank. In this position with the hard side against the fish, with fly, spinning or spiral casting guides located on the bottom, or regular casting guides on the top, many builders achieve what they believe to be the best overall position for fish fighting. It certainly offers the most power for fish fighting of any position. My suggestion is to try it for yourself, testing both for casting and fighting ability.

Hopefully, you are not too terribly confused at this point. Many builders will just go ahead and tell you where to locate the spine, based on their own preferences. I feel it is better for you to have a working knowledge of what the spine is and how it affects rod performance and have you decide for yourself where it should be located to suit your needs. Contrary to what some builders will tell you, it is impossible to locate the spine in the "wrong" position. I say test various positions for yourself, and then make the decision where to locate the spine by finding the position that allows your blank to come closest to doing what you want it to do.

Chapter 5

Grip, Handle and Seat Assembly

In many regards, the reel seat and handle or grip constitutes the business end of any fishing rod. This is your contact point with the rod and it also carries most of the stress and strain when fighting a fish. Guides can be rewrapped, tip-tops replaced, but the handle assembly, once mounted, is normally permanent. Before you begin this important task, it is necessary to have a plan in effect.

By now you have decided upon the type of rod you are going to build and selected and acquired your blank and components. The blank should be spined and you should decide how you wish to utilize the spine for your particular use. Mark the blank accordingly and lie it on a flat surface. Lie your grips and reel seat along the blank in the position in which you will be assembling them onto the rod. Put a mark with a grease pencil or Sharpie marker at the forward edge of where the total handle assembly will sit. Using fine sandpaper, gently scuff the blank throughout the area from the butt of your blank to the mark you made identifying the total area the handle will encompass. Now clean it thoroughly with alcohol.

Again lie it on a flat surface and again lie the handle components alongside it. This time make a mark at each point where one component ends and another one begins. In other words, you should mark out the area for each grip, the reel seat, the butt cap, etc. If you are building a fly rod you will have similar components but they may be arranged in a different order. A trolling rod intended for use with a uni-butt may require only the butt adapter and a grip. Either way, the assembly techniques are similar regardless of what type of rod you are building.

Synthetic Grips

Perhaps one of the easiest tasks to perform when building a rod is the installation of synthetic grips. Yet for many rod builders, installing EVA, hypalon or other various types of foam grips can be a nightmare. Problems when installing these grips usually stem from improper mounting technique. Once the proper technique is introduced, synthetic grips are easily and permanently installed with a minimum of fuss.

Before you begin the actual assembly of your blank and components, lay out your components in the order they will appear once assembled. Follow the instructions in the text for lay-out and measurement guidelines.

In the event that you need to alter a grip's length, to cut it, you must do this before mounting it to the rod. There are two easy ways to cut EVA grips. One is to wrap a band of masking tape around the point where you wish to make your cut and then use a single-edge razor blade or Xacto knife to slice around and through the grip. You can then round-over the cut edge with some sandpaper. If you have access to a lathe, you can mount the grip on a mandrel and place a small piece of tape at the point where the cut is to be made. Chuck it up and get it spinning and then use a piece of size D wrapping thread, held taut between your hands, as a cutting device. You simply lower the taut thread down against and into the grip and it will cut through it like butter! Round over the edge of the spinning grip with some sandpaper and you're done.

To easily and properly mount these grips you must select the proper adhesive and place it onto the blank in the correct location. The best adhesive is simple slow-cure epoxy of a fairly thin viscosity, which provides adequate working time and a permanent waterproof bond. Stay away from the 5-minute variety as you may find your grip "locking up" while it remains several inches from its intended location. Some builders like to augment any adhesive with some sort of lubricant, such as shaving cream. However, if the epoxy is properly placed on the blank, such lubricants are simply not needed.

The most common mistake when trying to mount these type of grips is improper location of the bonding adhesive. Far too many rod builders place the adhesive on the blank at the point where they wish the grip to ultimately sit. When this is done, the grip simply acts as a sort of squeegee, pushing the adhesive down and off the blank, leaving none between the grip and blank surface to act as both a lubricant during installation and a bonding agent when cured. Without the lubricating effect of the epoxy, tremendous force is often required to force the grip into position, and once there, it isn't likely to stay put through long hours of use and temperature changes.

You'll note in the photos on page 21 that we place our epoxy well above the intended final grip position, usually starting it several inches above where the grip's inside diameter matches the blank's outside diameter. This is done to allow the epoxy to coat both the surface of the blank *and* the inside of the grip. Once the inside of the grip is coated, the grip can be easily pushed into position with very little effort.

Once the grip has been brought down over the epoxy and turned several times to spread the epoxy completely inside, the fingers of one hand should squeeze tightly around the top of the grip. This acts as a seal at the top of the grip and allows the grip to be pushed, from the top edge, easily into place. The grip in the accompanying photos has an inner diameter of 1/4 inch, and the blank diameter where the grip was mounted is 1/2 inch. Using the technique shown, it was pushed into place with only a minimum of effort even though it had to be moved over a distance of 30 inches after it became tight on the blank. Without a coating of epoxy

inside the grip, it would have taken serious effort with a push board or pure muscle to force it into place.

Of course it stands to reason that a grip's inner diameter will only stretch so far. With this in mind, you can expect the best results by selecting a grip with an inner diameter that will need to be stretched at least a little, but not an overly large amount. Some of the softer grips can easily be made to fit blank diameters of nearly twice their inside diameter. Firmer grips may only expand enough to fit blank diameters of about 30% larger than their own inner diameters. If you find that one grip has an inside diameter too small to fit easily, and the next size up is simply too large, then it's time to get out the old reamer and do some work. Fortunately, this is rarely required.

Keep in mind that the act of pushing a grip onto a rod blank may result in it becoming slightly compressed in length. This is why it's a good idea to firmly stroke the grip from butt end to top end soon after it has been mounted. This action will return the grip to its original length. Notice also that in the photos the last few inches of mounting are done with the hand shifted to the bottom of the grip. This helps to stretch the grip back to its original length. If you know the fit will be extremely tight, you may even wish to cut it about 1/8" longer than the intended finished length. This tiny extra length will allow for a slight bit of compression that you may not be able to then extend on a really tight fit. At any rate, it's a wise idea to measure the grip after mounting to make sure it still conforms to the length you had intended.

Clean up is best done with solvent alcohol. And clean up will be necessary because there should be a thin film of epoxy all along the blank from a point above where the grip is mounted to the point where it was started. If no epoxy is present, then at some point the inside of the grip was not properly coated with epoxy and likely just squeegeed most of the epoxy down the blank. That thin film of epoxy you're hoping to see is proof that your grip is evenly and thoroughly coated all along its entire length.

Installing Cork Grips

Cork grips do not expand and stretch like the synthetic EVA and Hypolon varieties. They should be reamed and fitted to their approximate final location, lacking perhaps 1/2 inch or so of this position when dry-fit. The epoxy will lubricate the blank enough to allow the moving of the cork grip about 1/2 inch or so past this dry-fit location thereby allowing you to get it into the intended position with just a slight bit of effort.

Care must be taken when reaming cork grips. Unlike the synthetic foam grips, cork won't stretch, shrink or conform to make up for an imperfect fit. Common problems include over-reaming of the rear of the grip which neccesitates shimming of that area, and off-center reaming which throws the grip out of concentricity with the blank. Both of these maladies can be allayed by working slowly and carefully, checking for fit often. Try to match the taper you are cutting to that of the blank where the grip will ultimately sit.

Step 1: Drop the grip onto the blank and let it come to rest without any pressure. Make a mark at the point where it stops. You will want to place the bulk of your epoxy *above* this point, with only a little below.

Step 2: Mix and apply your 2-part epoxy to the blank. I recommend either a good slow-cure epoxy or Rod Bond from Trondak.

Step 3: Slowly bring the grip down and over the epoxy, turning it as you go to evenly spread the epoxy on the inside of the grip. As it tightens on the blank, wrap your thumb and forefinger securely around the top edge of the grip.

Step 4: Now begin to apply downward pressure and the grip will begin to slide easily into place.

Step 5: As you near the final resting place for your grip, move your hand to the bottom of the grip and "pull" into place. This will restore the original length of the grip which may have become compressed as it was being forced down the rod.

Step 6: Measure the grip and make sure it has returned to its original length. If not, pull it from the top edge, back up the rod blank until the original length is recovered.

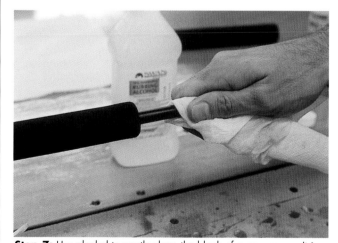

Step 7: Use alcohol to neatly clean the blank of excess epoxy. It is a good sign to see epoxy above the grip as this assures you that a coating of epoxy was maintained between the grip and the blank.

Work slowly and check the fit often. If the rear opening seems to be enlarging too fast, try putting more pressure on the forward part of the grip. As the hole begins to enlarge, switch to a larger reamer. By keeping the reamer large, close to the same size as the opening you are working on, you reduce the risk of creating an off-center opening.

On occasion, you will find that your grip ID may already be larger than the blank you are working on. If you cannot obtain a grip with a smaller ID, your only choice is to shim the area where the grip will sit, taking up the extra space. One very good method is to use heavy rod-winding thread, spiraled up and down the blank. If the grip opening is extremely large and the blank OD quite small, you may employ string or twine, also spiraled up and down the blank to take up the space. All this should be kept within reason however, as the more space you attempt to fill the greater the chance you will have a poor-fitting grip that could loosen or fail under use. With that in mind, if you find you have a very large opening to fill, I suggest obtaining another grip with the next smaller ID.

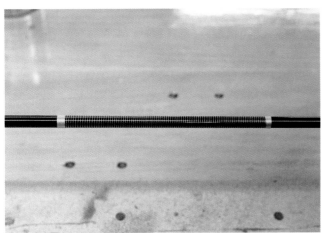

Once in awhile you may wish to use a grip which is just slightly over-sized for its intended position on the blank. A wrap of thread as shown will allow you to safely and securely mount such an oversized grip

Cork Tape

Some saltwater rods, most notably surf rods, are constructed with cork tape. This tape is actually a combination of cork and rubber particles joined together and backed with self-sticking adhesive. It works well on long-handled surf rods which often have large butt diameters and where the use of regular EVA or cork grips would dictate grips that are too long or too large in diameter for comfortable use.

If you are ordering cork tape and do not wish to purchase an entire 100-foot roll, figure the amount you need by measuring the length of the area that needs to be covered and multiplying that by 3. This simple formula should allow you purchase a length of tape that will be just a bit longer than what you will actually need, without creating much in the way of waste.

Begin by peeling off a portion of the backing that covers the self-stick adhesive. Don't remove all the backing at once, or the darn stuff will get stuck to everything in your work area! Just peel off a foot or so, then as you have wound up to that point, peel off some more. And so on. It will be necessary to start your tape at such an angle as to allow it to butt up against itself as you spiral it around the blank. Depending upon the diameter of your blank, this initial angle will vary. For this reason the easiest way to do this remains by trial and error. Start at an angle that looks good and make one revolution. If the tape winds on top of itself, you need to start with a greater angle. If you find that a large gap forms between the tape edges, then start with a shallower angle. The adhesive on the tape will easily let go, at least for now, and allow you to reposition the starting angle of the tape so don't be afraid that you won't be able to remove this small portion. Keep trying until you get the angle that will allow the tape to spiral around and keep edge against edge on each revolution.

When you have finished spiraling the tape around the entire distance to be covered, temporarily bind down the edges with masking tape. Cut the ends off clean and straight with a single-edge razor blade. Try to find a smooth, very flat area and roll the tape-wrapped assembly on it. I sometimes use a block of wood on top of the tape-wrap to press and roll the tape-wrapped blank against such a smooth, flat surface. This "sets" the cork tape on the blank and ensures it will stay put for many long seasons.

Now you must make locking thread wraps that will bind the tape edges in place permanently. (See Chapter 7 on guide wrapping for the technique on making these wraps.) These wraps don't need to be long, but must be made quite close to the edge. Some builders like to use the cork tape for foregrips on these rods as well. In such a case, you will likely wish to extend the locking wrap from the tape edge down onto the blank for a smooth transition. To do this, you must carefully sand the edge of the tape to a bit of a taper. Once that is done, you can start your wrap on the blank, then wrap towards the tape edge. As your thread contacts the tape edge, it will slowly start to climb up onto it, packing back against itself as it climbs. (If you experience trouble getting the thread to climb up onto the tape, you need to sand the edge to a shallower angle.) Once the thread is on top of the tape edge, continue it to your desired length and complete the wrap.

These locking thread wraps should be finished in the normal manner which is fully explained in Chapter 8 on thread-wrap finishing.

Seat Selection and Installation

You should select the size reel seat that will accommodate the reel you will be using as well as be comfortable in your hand. Too many rod builders select their seat size based on how it will mate to the blank. That is not the way to go about this important decision. Obviously the seat needs to be large enough to fit over the blank at the point where it will ultimately be located. Beyond that, it must open far enough to accept the reel you intend on using and be comfortable in the hand. During my own rod-building career, many of my customers were delighted to have a complete set of different sized rods only with each featuring the same-sized reel seat. Sort of like a set of golf clubs where each club performs a different task, but all have the same size grip. This results in greater comfort and ease of use for the angler, although it means the builder must devise a way to shim the reel so that it can fit on a blank which may be quite a bit smaller than the seat.

The easiest way is to create shims or bushings from masking tape. Geez, I hate to even mention that method, but it is so widely used and accepted by both commercial and custom builders that I will at least give it a mention. It works reasonably well, but I believe a good custom rod deserves better.

If you like the speed of using tape to make arbors or bushings, you might try something called "fiberglass drywall tape". It is sold at most hardware or building supply stores. It is comprised of a grid of fiberglass strands and can be wound around the blank until the seat fits snugly. Most of the time this tape is sold in rolls that are at least a couple inches wide. In order to account for the difference in diameter, due to blank taper between the forward and rearward seat-mounting area, you may wish to cut the tape into 1-inch strips. This will allow you to make two separate arbors, using more tape on the forward arbor than the rear, effectively leveling out the blank taper and creating a better fit for the reel seat. Although the tape is coated with a self adhesive, you should "tack" the edge to the blank with a small piece of masking tape, and again "tack" the final overwrap of tape to itself with another piece of masking tape. If you don't, you will find it unwinding and becoming unwieldy as you attempt to slide the seat down over it.

If the fit is close, I like to make bushings from rod-wrapping thread. To even out any difference created by the blank's taper, I might find myself using 3 or 4 layers on the rear bushing, and 4 or 5 layers of thread on the forward bushing. Using size D or even E rod-wrapping thread makes this task much quicker to perform. Some builders use the same idea on blanks and seats that require a larger space to be filled by utilizing twine or string in the same fashion as the thread mentioned above. Fine, that works well too. But try to be neat with your wrapping.

Shimming a butt end of an IGFA trolling or stand-up blank to fit a Uni-butt can be done with thread or drywall tape. Most of the time these instances only require a very small space to be filled and either of the previously mentioned materials will work very well.

My preferred material for taking up larger spaces is a solid, rigid material known as brick-foam. If you like, you can purchase it from your blank and component supplier in ready-to-fit arbor kits from Fuji or Pacific Bay. The outer diameter of these arbors/bushings is chosen to match the size seat you are using, while the inside diameter must

Reel seat bushings or arbors can be made from a variety of materials. Light, rigid materials are best. Shown here are arbors made from cork, "brick foam" and bands of large-diameter wrapping thread. Fiberglass drywall tape is another option and should be considered a better choice than masking tape.

In this instance, we have fitted "brick foam" arbors to the blank. They have been affixed to the blank with epoxy and the seat will now be mounted.

be enlarged by boring or reaming. If you have a lathe, they can be bored to closely match the ID of the blank where they will reside, a final fitting with a tapered reamer gives the final, perfect fit. Without a lathe or drill, you are faced with hand reaming. It's not such a bad job, but does require careful reaming and fitting to ensure you don't over-ream one end of the bushing, or get the opening off-center.

My suggestion is to use drywall tape, thread or string wraps if you only need to take up small differences in size, say less than 3/16 inches and to use the brick-foam arbors if you need to take up spaces greater than that.

If you are the creative type, you will no doubt find other materials that will work well as bushings or arbors. The important thing when taking up large spaces between the reel seat and the blank is to select a material that is light yet rigid. As an example, cork makes an excellent material for reel-seat bushings. It is easily reamed to fit the blank and seat and is very light yet fairly rigid.

The type material you choose for making reel-seat arbors or bushings will depend upon how much space you need to fill, and what materials you either have on hand or are willing to acquire. All of those mentioned above will work equally well. Try to achieve a fit between your arbors/bushings and seat that is just barely snug, but not terribly tight. Scuff the inside of the reel seat, or Uni-butt ferrule, which you are planning to mount and then clean it thoroughly on the inside with alcohol.

The seat is mounted with epoxy and excess glue removed from the area. The fore grip is mounted in the same manner as the butt grip we mounted earlier. Make sure to clean excess epoxy from the joints between grips and seat. Epoxy can continue to seep out for about an hour so check back and continue to remove any excess until no more is evident.

The best adhesive for mounting your reel seat will be either a good slow-cure two-part epoxy, or U-40 Rod Bond. Thoroughly coat the surfaces and sides of your arbors or bushings with the adhesive and slide the seat down over the assembly, rotating it as you do so. (Make sure that your final position has the seat in line with the axis where you have planned to mount your guides. More than one rod builder has carefully mounted a seat only to return later and realize he forgot to line it up with the axis where the guides are supposed to go!) Carefully clean up any epoxy that may have squeezed out of the joint with a rag or cloth saturated with alcohol. More epoxy may seep out of the assembly for a few minutes so it is important to keep an eye on things and clean up any that does escape. Otherwise you will wind up with an ugly glue line on the outside of the assembly.

The fore grip, if your particular type of rod requires one, is mounted in the same manner as the rear grip. Again, be careful and watch for any adhesive that gets squeezed out of the assembly and clean it off immediately.

If you desire to use a winding check, you may install it now, tacking it against the foregrip with a few spots of epoxy applied with a toothpick. Clean up any excess and set the entire handle assembly aside to dry overnight.

Chapter 6

Guide Placement

Okay, you've spined your blank, built your handle and now you're ready to wrap the guides. But wait, how do you know where to put them? The first inclination for most rod builders is to try and acquire some sort of spacing chart from a book, catalog or blank manufacturer. This is, perhaps, the biggest mistake you can make when attempting to build a fishing rod, particularly if you want to achieve the highest level of performance and fishability from it.

So what's wrong with the measurements given on the various spacing charts, you say? Plenty. First of all, no spacing chart has any idea what type guides you will be using, the length of your handle and the particular action or taper of the blank in your possession. All of these things factor into the proper spacing of line guides if you are maximizing the performance potential of your rod. I have only one thing to say about spacing charts—**Don't use them!**

Okay you say, just how do I go about locating these guides if I don't use somebody else's spacing measurements? Simple. You figure your own spacing by some test casting and static distribution test. It's fairly easy, fun to accomplish and will assure you that you are getting the most out of your new rod blank. And best of all, once you learn how to do it, you can easily and accurately figure the guide spacing for any rod blank you will ever come across.

Let's start by explaining that your objective in terms of line guides is to use the fewest number of guides possible that will still provide adequate stress distribution for the blank, and keep the line flowing smoothly along the curvature of the blank during periods of maximum stress. By now you understand the importance of keeping weight to a minimum if you are going to have the most efficient rod possible. Hence, you want to use the fewest guides possible to get the job done. Determining how many guides to use can only be determined by the static distribution test however, and that only after determining where we are going to locate our first, or butt, guide and tipmost guide. Let's get started.

Spinning Rods

In the old days, we heard much concerning the "choking" of the line as it left the spinning-reel spool. Turns out, much of that was just myth. The line must ultimately pass through the tip-top, usually with a small ring. Getting the size of the guides down quickly, instead of a gradual drop as favored in the old days, saves weight, reduces air resistance, and can actually increase casting distance.

The engineers at Fuji Kogyo have proven that smaller-ringed, higher-framed guides actually increase casting distance on spinning rods. Within the past few years they have

also tested the theory that you need to reduce your guide sizes quickly, within the first three of four guides, to the smallest size you will be using at any point on the rod. They call this the Fuji New Concept Guide Spacing System and I am a believer. For instance, in the old days, we might have used a guide set-up that looked something like this in ring sizes: 30mm, 25mm, 20mm, 16mm, 12mm, 10mm, 8mm and 8mm top. Now, we suddenly find that using a set-up consisting of: 30mm, 20mm, 12mm, 8mm, 8mm, 8mm, 8mm and 8mm top actually cast as far or farther than the traditional method and reduces overall weight by a significant amount. Casting distance is enhanced rather than hindered. The rod moves through the air better, fatigues the angler less and just plain feels better. In fact, the only question seems to be why did it take so long for us to figure this out? Thanks to Fuji, we have recently seen another giant leap in rod performance.

The Choke Guide

With that said, this is where I am going to break with traditional guide placement methods and take you into newly chartered waters with the system that has worked best for

Using the edge of a table as a straightedge to determine the choke guide position on spinning rod.

me. It combines our initial test casting with some aspects of the New Concept Guide Spacing System. Take your rod, with reel attached, and lie it flat on a table or the floor. Notice that the reel spool is angled up a few degrees towards the rod tip. Either eyeball or run a string directly through the centerline of the reel spool and continue until it intersects the rod blank. Mark this point of intersection. This is where you will locate the choke guide, which is the first guide of the smallest ring diameter you plan on using. On most spinning rods, this will likely be either a 7mm, 8mm or 10mm. From that point to the tip, you will use guides which are identical in frame height and ring size as that choke guide. Towards the butt, you will locate, in progressively larger sizes, the guides which will lead back to the butt guide. Size these guides by choosing ring and frame sizes that will put their outermost edges at or near that imaginary line you ran a minute ago between the reel spool centerline and the point of intersection with the rod blank. Depending upon the size of the reel, the choke guide will usually be the fourth guide *from* the butt end. On very small ultra-light rods it may be the third guide, while on really large saltwater rods, it may be the fifth guide. The upcoming static distribution test will determine which it will be, but it should always be sized as the smallest ringed guide you plan on using. From the choke guide, eyeball a few guides of the same size as the choke guide on out to the tip-most guide. It might take 1, 2, 3 or more, depending upon total rod length. Aft of the choke guide, you will place 2, 3 or perhaps 4 guides of increasingly larger sizes towards the butt guide, again in a progressive manner. The closer you can get the outermost edge of the guide ring to that imaginary line you ran from the reel center line to the point where it intersected with the blank, the better. Use of higher-frame guides will facilitate this to a great extent.

The total number of guides to use will usually run about one more than the number of feet in length as the rod blank. In other words, a 6-foot rod will take 7 guides plus a tip-top. This number is not set in stone however, and will ultimately be determined by our static distribution test run after our casting test. I want to point out, that the New Concept System generally requires the use of 1 or 2 more guides than the traditional method, which would seem to contradict what I said earlier about using the fewest number of guides possible in order to achieve better rod efficiency. Actually, once you understand that with the New Concept System, we are using smaller guides than with the traditional methods, you will find that we are still arriving at a guide set-up that weighs far less than what we would have when using the more traditional "gradual drop" guide set-up.

Now you are going to have to do some test casting in order to determine the proper location of the butt guide. Your handle is in place, so it is a simple matter to affix the reel you plan on using and taping the selected guides in place in order to test cast the rig. Tape the guides securely to the rod with a few bands of masking tape. Now go outside to an open area and cast the rod with the reel, line size and

approximate casting weight which you plan on using when the rod is finished. Walk off the distance after the cast, keeping a written record of both the casting distance and the distance from the tip-top that the butt guide is located. Then try moving the guide up an inch towards the tip and make a couple of casts there. Record the results. Move it back from the original location about an inch towards the reel and cast again. Record the results. Don't be afraid to move the guide well away from the original location, both from and towards the tip-top during the testing, always recording both the casting distance and the measurement of the butt guide from the tip-top. At some point you will find a position where the

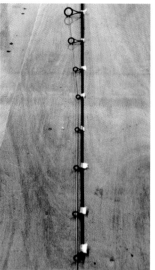

Spinning guide placement via the "New Guide Concept" system (left). Ultra high-frame guides control and gather the unfurling line and quickly bring it down to the choke guide. From there it is carried out to the tip-top by means of small-ring, low-frame guides. This system results in less overall weight being added to the blank thus reducing rod efficiency to a lesser degree than older systems (right) where large-ring guides were used in a "cone-of-flight" set-up. Distance is as good or better with the "New Guide Concept" system.

On the left are two guides, both holding #16 rings. The higher of the two is from Fuji's "Concept" series of rod guides. It is designed to allow the unfurling line from a spinning reel to make a direct flight path to the choke guide without deviating from its natural course. On the right is a #20 spinning guide. Notice that is about the same height as the highest #16. Sometimes, using a larger ring will get you the extra height you need, but nearly always at some expense of extra weight. Never be afraid to mix, match or choose guide frame styles and heights in order to achieve the desired result.

rod casts the farthest, and feels the best. If you want to fine-tune the butt guide placement even more, you can continue test-casting while using various-sized butt guides. Maybe try one size larger and one size smaller than the original and repeat the tests. Again, at some point, you will arrive at a butt-guide size and placement that will provide the greatest casting distance. Circle that measurement in your records. This will be your approximate butt-guide location for the finished rod.

Let me again stress that you are attempting to achieve the greatest results with the least amount of material. Suffice it to say, you hope to make use of the smallest-diameter butt guide (lightest) that offers the best distance. As you try larger guides and the distance no longer increases, stay with the size that offered the last increase. Beyond that point, a larger butt guide will only add weight, not distance.

Assuming you have now decided upon the optimum placement for your butt guide, you will want to run the line from the reel through the guides and out to the tip-top. Attach the end of the line to a solid object and holding the handle, flex the rod generously. Try to emulate the line flow of the rod in the photo below. You are trying to achieve a nice, even line flow which matches the curvature of the blank as closely as possible. Granted, the New Concept Guide System tends to make this a bit more difficult, but once you understand the concept, you should be able to visualize what we are shooting for. Again, consult the pictures on page 26 to see what we want, and what we do not want. If there are long expanses of flat spots, where the line doesn't flow with the flex of the blank, you will need to adjust the spacing and/or add another guide. (During static distribution, the choke guide should remain in its original location, no matter how much you move the other guides. The butt guide, the choke guide and the tip-most guides are set, and proper static distribution is achieved by moving the guides in between.)

Notice how the line follows the very same curvature as the blank when under a load. This is an excellent example of what you want to achieve when locating guides along the rod blank. It is important that the guides be located properly in order to distribute stress evenly along the blank and to keep the blank from being forced into any sort of unnatural bend or stress.

If you hit on perfect line flow on your first attempt, try removing a guide and see if you can still manage to achieve a nice line flow along the blank's curvature. Remember the fewer guides you are able to use, while maintaining good line flow, the better the rod will perform.

Once you arrive at a guide-spacing set-up that looks good, go back outside and do some more casting. You may need to adjust the butt guide slightly, and if so the other guides between the butt and choke guide will need to be adjusted slightly as well. The end result will be a perfect marriage between rod and guides that offers the greatest casting distance and the lightest rod possible.

Of course, all this requires a considerable bit more work than just copying guide spacing off a chart or from a factory rod you already own. But trust me, it's worth it. After the initial effort and testing, much of what we have gone through here will become second hand and either will not have to be repeated or can be quickly accomplished on future rods. Test casting and proper guide placement is a big part of true rod building. It also separates the rod builders from the rod assemblers, who are content to copy and achieve acceptable, but not spectacular, results.

Fly Rods

Determining guide spacing for fly rods is much like determining the spacing for spinning rods except that it's actually quicker and easier since you're not dealing with line peeling off in revolutions from the reel spool. Some basics remain the same however. You want to use the minimum number of guides that will still provide adequate stress distribution and good line flow along the blank.

Again, the tip-most guide should not be located farther back than 4 or 5 inches from the tip. In fact, I'd almost go so far as to suggest you just put it 4 inches behind the tip and leave it at that. This goes for light-line rods as well as heavier line rods. You will want this guide to be sized so that it is of the same ring diameter as the ring in your tip-top.

The butt, or stripping guide as it is usually referred to on these rods, must be far enough ahead of the reel to prevent the shooting line from having to negotiate a sharp angle, but close enough to allow you to make use of the power in the butt section when fighting a nice fish. I suggest holding the rod by the grip as if you were fishing it, with your arm held so that your upper arm and forearm are at a 90-degree angle to one another, rod positioned horizontally. Now with the other arm, reach up to the rod blank as if you were going to grasp the line to start a cast. Don't under- or over-reach, just normally and comfortably reach up to the point where you normally grasp the line. Mark the point where your hand contacts the rod. In most cases, the best stripping guide position will be about an inch or two beyond that point.

Now a word about stripping guide sizes. In most cases, the stripping guides on commercially made rods are too small. You will realize better casting by using a stripping guide that is roughly one ring size larger than what you find on comparable line weight rods built commercially. You may also find that using a high-frame style spinning guide reduces line slap against the rod during casting. Most commercially made fly rods utilize standard casting style guides as stripping guides. You can too, but I'd at least throw in a high-frame spinning guide during the tests. In either case, use one size larger than what you see on the factory rods. This might mean using a #12 on lighter-line rods, say about 2- through 6-weights. Or a #16 on 7- through 9-weights and a larger #20 on the big 10- through 15-weights. Don't be afraid to try larger sizes and a variety of frame styles. A little extra time spent testing various set-ups now will result in years of pleasurable rod performance down the line.

Now that you have your tip-most guide located, and the stripping guide has been positioned about an inch beyond the point mentioned above, you can position, by eye, the rest of the guides between those two. Again, it should be done in a progressive manner, with distances between the guides increasing as you move towards the butt of the rod. A good rule of thumb concerning the number of guides you will need on a fly rod, is to use the same number of guides as the number of feet in length of the rod blank. A 9-foot fly rod would take 9 guides plus a top, etc. This number may need to be adjusted during the static distribution test, but most times you will find that at most, you will only need to either add or delete one guide to get the optimum number for your particular rod.

Once you have taped the guides in place, go outside and with the reel and line you plan on using on the rod, do some test casting. Move the stripping guide up an inch or so at a time, and then back an inch or so at a time. Within a few dozen casts, you will arrive at a location that seems to offer the best distance and feel. Mark this location as your stripping guide location.

Now go back inside and run a line through the guides and out past the top. Fasten the line to a stable object and flex the rod. Adjust the guides so that you are able to maintain a nice, even line flow, that corresponds with the curvature of the blank. Most probably, you will have to move a few and in some cases you may have to add one additional guide if you cannot achieve a decent line flow along the blank. In the event that your initial spacing yields a nice flow right off the bat, try taking out one guide and respacing again. If you can get good line flow with one less guide, so much the better. The more guides you use, the easier it will be to achieve this good line flow, but more guides add weight and hurt rod performance. So the idea remains to try and achieve optimum stress distribution and line flow with the fewest guides possible.

What about locating guides on the ferrule? Most fly rods are of multi-piece design and ferrules are a matter of fact. It neither helps nor hinders rod performance if guides need to be located on, or away from, the ferrules. Placing guides directly on top of female ferrules is perfectly acceptable. About the only thing you have to watch out for is the male ferrule section on rods with tip-over-butt ferrules. Any

A static distribution test should always be run before making a final decision on guide placement. The idea is to have the line follow the curvature of the blank while using as few guides as is possible. Here a fly rod is pressured in order to test guide placement. Notice how the line flows along the same curvature as the blank. Flat spots have been eliminated by adjusting spacing and/or adding additional guide/s.

guide located near the male ferrule section must be located far enough behind it so that the female ferrule section can fully seat on the male section. My advice is to leave at least an inch clearance behind the fully seated edge of the female ferrule when locating any guide near the male ferrule.

One last guide spacing item to be addressed on fly rods concerns the technique of adding an additional stripping guide to increase casting distance. This additional guide however, does not play into the usual set-up you have already determined by your casting and static tests. Instead, it is added *after* you have already determined the optimum guide spacing for the rod as directed above and it is located 3 or 4 inches ahead (towards the tip) of your butt stripping guide. The idea behind this technique is to straighten out and better direct the line flow during casting by having two butt stripping guides placed close to each other, thereby reducing the tendency of the line to "overshoot" the first stripping guide. In actual tests, this technique has proven to add a measurable increase in casting distance! If you decide to try it, here's what you'll want to do. Go ahead and securely tape the other guides in the positions you have determined by our earlier casting and static distribution tests. Add one additional stripping guide at a point about 4 inches beyond (towards the tip) the first stripping guide. This additional stripping guide should be the same size as the guide which was originally your second stripper. Now go out and do some test casting. If you do not find it adds any additional distance, scrap it. In the likely event that you find it does result in a casting distance increase, you'll have to decide whether or not to add it to your guide set-up. Some folks don't like the unconventional look it gives the rod. Others are always out for what works best. This is a decision you will have to make for yourself.

Casting/Trolling/Boat Rods

On the rod types we have previously discussed, there has been no chance that the line will come into contact with the blank when it is bent under the strain of a large fish. Not so with casting and trolling rods, where the simple act of placing the guides on top of the rod means that careful placement will be required if you are to keep the line off the blank during periods when the rod is severely bent under load. And this is, in fact, a major concern when determining guide placement for any rod where the guides are located on top of the blank rather than underneath it.

To begin, we must determine the proper placement of our butt guide. It will be very helpful to have the reel you plan on using on the rod in order to do this. For the time being, tape some guides on the blank in a progressive fashion. Use about the same number of guides as the blank's length. For a 6-footer use 6 and for a 7-footer use 7. This number will be adjusted later. With a full reel spool, you will want to have the line come off the far side of the spool (either side, it doesn't matter) and down through your butt guide and on out the remainder of the guides and top. Attach the end of the line to a heavy object and holding the rod by its handle, put a decent bend in it. The trick here is another one of compromise. You want the line to travel as freely as possible without being choked into that butt guide. In other words, you don't want the line to enter the butt guide through a sharp angle. Naturally you can eliminate this by positioning the guide farther up the rod, but then when the rod is under load you may find that the line will contact either the blank or the foregrip before entering the reel. That's no good. If you find yourself in this position, move the butt guide back down the rod a bit until it clears the area between itself and the reel. If you need to hold the rod by the foregrip for your specific type of fishing, allow for that as well by positioning the guide so that it keeps the line high enough where it will not cut into your hand or is high enough for you to cross-wrap it on the spool with non level-wind reels. If you cannot seem to reach a good compromise, you need to adjust the size and height of the butt guide. A higher butt guide allows you a bit more freedom in placement options, just as a butt guide with a larger ring allows you to place the guide a bit closer to the reel without choking line flow.

Again, the trick is to use the smallest and lightest guides that will get the necessary job done. Don't be afraid to move up a few sizes in guide size and height to get the job done, but remember that the bigger the guide, the more weight the rod is carrying. Unfortunately there is no hard and fast rule for selecting proper butt guide sizing. It's one of those things that you will only discover by trial and error. I will offer this one suggestion however, and that is that most commercially made rods use a butt guide which I feel is about one size too small. With that in mind, you can look at any factory-made rod that is close in size and scope to what you are building and start your testing with a butt guide that is one size larger than what you find on it. At least it gives you a place to start.

On rods with the guides located on top, such as this freshwater casting rod, the line should not touch the blank when under load. Use of higher-frame guides, or lower-frame guides in greater quantity, is the answer.

Once you have determined the optimum butt guide location, you can begin to play with the other guides. Just as with spinning and fly rods, you are trying to arrange the guides in such a way as to keep the line flowing in an arc which closely matches that of the flexed rod. In order to do this, and keep the line from contacting the blank, you will likely find that you must use 1 or 2 more guides on a casting type rod than you would on the same length spinning or fly rod. That's okay. The only thing you need to decide now is exactly how you want to keep the line off the blank—with lower-frame guides which reduce the tendency of the rod to torque when line pressure is applied but which requires more of them, or with higher-frame guides which allow you to use fewer guides to keep the line off the blank but which will increase the tendency to torque and twist when under load. I'm not making this very easy for you, am I?

The decision on which type of guide set-up to use can be simplified somewhat by the power of the rod with which you are working. If you are building something along the lines of a freshwater casting rod, I suggest using lower-frame guides, at least out near the tip and adding however many it takes to keep the line away from the blank. Smaller guides in most modern styles are fairly light and should not affect the performance of the blank to any appreciable degree. They also offer less air resistance and a reduction in the tendency for the blank tip to twist under load. These things add up to a rod that will be more pleasant to cast with, the very purpose for which the rod is likely being built. On heavier, more powerful rods like boat or offshore trolling rods, lean towards higher-framed guides which will allow you to use perhaps a guide or two less. Yes, the higher frame may increase the tendency of a rod to twist when under load, but on these heavier, stiffer blanks this tendency is on the entire blank and is held steady by the angler or a gimbal nock in a fighting chair or harness. On lighter rods such as those mentioned previously, line moving through such higher-framed guides will twist the tip around even if the angler holds the butt section upright. To review, try smaller, lower framed guides in higher numbers on the lighter casting rods, and fewer, but higher-framed guides on heavy, powerful trolling and boat rods.

There is one other alternative in guide placement for casting type rods and it involves spiraling the guides around the rod blank so that most of the guides are then placed along the underside of the rod a la spinning- and fly-rod style. This idea came about as a result of long downrigger and live bait rods with light, fast tips. These rods required so many guides on the tip area to keep the line away from the blank that some enterprising angler/rod builder reasoned that if the line could be run along the bottom of the rod he wouldn't have to use as many guides. And he was right. In the past few years this concept has been extended to many other casting-style rods as well, up to and including heavier offshore live bait and trolling rods. Regardless of what you might think of such a set-up, the fact is that it works remarkably well provided the concept is well executed.

The only real problem with these "spiral" guide set-ups lies in how you get the line from the reel, which is on top of the rod, around and to the underside of the rod without completely undermining good casting or line retrieval qualities.

A "spiral wrap" can be used on longer casting rods to keep the number of line guides to a minimum. By taking the line from the top of the rod around to the bottom, the line will not touch the rod, the rod will be more stable and you may be able to reduce the overall number of guides needed.

Luckily it can be done. For many years I had settled on a spiral method which set the butt guide location as in the earlier discussion on casting-style rods. Then I used three additional guides to get the line around the blank. I spaced them about 3 or 4 inches apart and at 60, 120 and 180 degrees around the blank. It worked very, very well on the live-bait rods I was building and was decent on rods used mostly for casting. But it was a friend and fellow rod builder, Ralph O'Quinn, who exposed me to a spiral set-up he had developed which worked even better, particularly on rods which were destined for casting duty. Ralph eliminated the sharp contact points of line against those first 3 or 4 guides by routing the line in a straight path directly from the reel to the first underside (180-degree position) guide. Then he came back toward the reel with 2 or 3 more guides that were offset the necessary amount so as not to interfere with that straight path the line was now traveling. The result was a set-up that required the line to make only one course correction, and a fairly minor one at that. The problem in many builders' eyes, however, was that such a method required the butt guide to be placed offset, rather than straight up at the 0-degree position. They reasoned that with a level-wind reel the line would pile up heavier on one side of the spool, towards the side of the offset guide. But their reasoning was, and is, flawed. Line will indeed pile up heavier to one side of the spool if the line is moved far enough off the rod centerline, particularly outside of the spool's width. But with Ralph's set-up, the slight offset of the butt guide barely moves the line a few millimeters from actual rod centerline. As such, it is a non-issue as far as line retrieval on the spool is concerned.

This spiral guide set-up for casting-style rods is gaining new converts every day. It keeps the line off the blank and yet results in the use of far fewer guides out near the tip area, which translates into better performance. Casting attributes are not harmed if executed properly, so there is really very little keeping this set-up from becoming the standard casting set-up one day in the future. Obviously, due to the nature of current guide designs, heavy offshore trolling rods which utilize roller guides are not good candidates for this spiral treatment. But nearly any other type of rod which can utilize ringed guides is a very likely candidate for spiral guide placement. I encourage you to experiment with this idea. With a bit of trial and error, I think you will adopt it as your favorite casting rod set-up.

For those of you who were hoping for some sort of chart listing spacing measurements and guide sets, this chapter has likely left you confused and disappointed. But if you want to understand how to intelligently craft the spacing and guide selection for any blank, it will put you on the right path. It will allow you to optimize guide style and placement for any blank through the knowledge of what must be achieved and how to accomplish this. It will put you a step further from being a simple rod-wrapper and one step closer to becoming a true rod builder. It will also help you to build a much better performing fishing rod.

Chapter 7

Guide Prep and Wrapping

The wrapping of line guides to a rod blank is what most people think of when someone talks about "rod building". Although wrapping is perhaps the easiest facet of building a rod, it also gives many newcomers fits and has caused more than one aspiring rod builder to throw up his hands and swear off the craft entirely. Fortunately, almost anyone can become proficient at wrapping with a bit of practice and some helpful guidance.

Guide Prep

Before we can begin wrapping, however, we must prep our guides. As supplied, line guides have a rather blunt edge on the end of each foot and the wrapping thread will not want to climb over it easily. Thus, we need to reshape each foot edge so that the thread can make an easy transition onto the foot. There are several ways to do this and it may seem like some sort of grinder would be the easiest way, I hesitate to suggest this because the resulting ground guide foot is usually burned, coarse, de-tempered and covered with sharp burrs on the underside. Unless you're an old pro at this, let's just start with a simple file.

There are two important things to keep in mind here: most files cut in only one direction and the guide being worked on must be solidly supported. Use the edge of a vise, a block of wood or something similar to rest the guide on, with the edge of the foot protruding out over the edge of the vise or wooden block. File slowly with *long,* smooth forward strokes, resisting the temptation to drag the file back across the foot. Doing so will only dull the file—remember the forward stroke is the cutting stroke. Work on the top edge of the foot, bring it down lower and lower until the edge at the end of the foot is a very shallow, almost sharp angle. On your first attempts you will likely decide to stop too soon, and later will notice the difficulty in getting the thread to climb up onto the guide foot when wrapping. Most rod builders do a better guide prep job the second time around, once they see what it is they are trying to accomplish and what it takes to achieve that shallow angle.

Any burrs or extremely sharp edges on the bottom of the guide feet must be removed by sanding with fine emery or crocus cloth. You do not want sharp cutting edges coming into contact with your blank. Once wrapped, and after the rod has flexed repeatedly, these edges can begin to cut into the blank, fracturing it and resulting in rod failure at a later date. Poor guide foot prep is the leading cause of failure in custom rods.

Finally, with your guide feet filed to a shallow edge and all burrs and sharp edges removed, you should check to see that each guide will sit perfectly flat on the blank surface.

Use fine-nose pliers to gently bend and shape the guide feet so that they sit flat on the blank. Wrapping tension is cumulative and if only a small area or point of a guide foot actually contacts the surface there will be a tremendous amount of pressure placed on a very small area of the blank's surface. Again, failure can be the result. Think of someone standing on your hand while wearing a flat-soled shoe as opposed to a woman's high-heeled shoe. You do not want all the wrapping pressure concentrated on one small point, so make sure the guide foot sits flat and contacts the blank across its entire length.

Guide prep may be the least fun part of rod building, but it is actually one of, if not the most important part, of the entire process. Proper guide prep will make your wrapping tasks easier and will ensure the rod you build will not fail due to poor workmanship on your part. Spend the extra time to do it right the first time around.

Thread Tension

The tendency for most rod builders is to use far too much thread tension when wrapping. Remember that thread tension is cumulative and increases with each additional wind. It does not take much in the way of thread tension to securely hold a guide to the blank. Remember as well, that your wraps will also be coated with some type of finish, effectively locking things in place. There is no accurate method for measuring wrapping tension other than to wrap one guide and check to see if you can move it under the completed wrap. In fact, you should be able to move it with slight sideways pressure once wrapped. This serves two purposes: first it allows you to align the guides once they are wrapped and it also ensures that you have not used excessive wrapping tension which can often damage the blank.

Obviously, larger, heavy-duty rods, such as those meant for big game offshore fishing, will require more wrapping tension than what is required for an ultra-light spinning rod. Keep in mind the type of rod you are working with, the job it is expected to do and the wall thickness of the particular blank you are working with, and wrap accordingly. This may be a bit vague, but think in terms of wrapping "snug" not "tight" and you should be okay.

Wrapping

Perhaps the biggest mistake the novice makes with regard to wrapping the guides is heavy handedness. Smooth, even guide wraps are the result of a light touch, not extreme effort. If things aren't going well, grasping the blank tighter, forcing the blank down into the "V" blocks or increasing tension on the thread will only make things worse. For the remainder of this chapter, I want you to keep in mind that a light touch coupled with a bit of patience is the answer to making neat, quick guide wraps. Now let's get started.

The very best way to affix the guides to the blank is with narrow strips of masking tape. Either purchase some very narrow masking tape or simply tear or cut some narrow tape strips from your existing tape so that when you tape the guide to the blank about 1/2 of the guide's outer foot/feet are exposed for wrapping. Affix the tape to the guide foot/feet and set the guide down on the blank with one hand, using your free hand to push the tape onto the sides of the blank. It is not necessary to wrap the tape around the blank, which only makes it harder to remove later. Just push the tape into contact with the sides of the blank and move on to the next one. It is not imperative to get the guides into perfect alignment at this time, but it is suggested that you get them as close as you can. Final alignment will be made after the guides are wrapped.

If you are using the simple wrapping set-up shown in the photos, you will have your thread coming onto the rod blank from behind and then over the top. In the event that you are using a different wrapping set-up, your thread may be coming from below and in front. In either case, the wrapping sequence is pretty much the same but if your thread comes onto the rod from the front, you will need to adjust your perspective if the sequence is to make any sense.

In order to make your first few wraps a bit easier, I suggest wrapping a piece of masking tape completely around the blank at the point where you wish your guide wrap to begin. This provides you with a makeshift "edge" to work against and will make your first wraps much easier. Bring your thread over and around the top of the blank. Make a complete wrap with the tag end being brought around and to the inside (that means towards the guide) of this first revolution. Holding the tag end with one hand, rotate the rod blank towards you slightly and with the same hand that is rotating the rod, use a finger to gently push the oncoming thread over the standing thread to form a locking "X". At this point, many novice rod builders will encounter difficulty as they continue to rotate the rod and find that the rod spins independently and the thread just sits there and slips on top of the rod. For that reason, after you have nudged the oncoming thread over the top of the standing thread, stop for second and spiral the tag end around the blank 2 or 3 times. Now you may resume rotating the rod, making sure that on each revolution the oncoming thread is wrapping over the standing thread. After about 3 revolutions the wrap will be locked in place and you can release the tag end which you had spiraled around the blank. Use your thumbnail or a blunt instrument to push the thread back against the tape edge so that it will square. This will make it easier to complete the wrap. Continue wrapping until you have 5 or 6 winds of thread over the tag end and then carefully cut the tag end free. It is not necessary to cut the tag end flush with the wrap, as it will be completely wrapped over. Just get reasonably close.

If you have managed to get through the wrapping start and thread lock-in, on the first attempt, give yourself a pat on the back. It's not hard to do, but beginners usually have problems trying to get both hands and all fingers working together to achieve the same end. If you did have trouble, cut or unwind the thread and try again. Follow the photos starting on page 33 closely and you should get the hang of it within a few tries.

After you have gotten the thread started and locked-in, you can begin the task of winding the thread up onto the guide foot. At this point you will know if you spent enough time properly dressing the foot. A shallow angle allows the thread to climb easily onto the guide foot while a blunt edge will make this harder, but not impossible. As the thread begins to climb onto the foot, you will find that it also begins to pack tighter at that point and that the wrap seems to be growing faster on the bottom of the rod, away from the guide foot. This is normal. On each revolution, or at least after every few, use your thumbnail to push the thread on the bottom of the rod back far enough so that the wrap continues in an even line. If you are having problems with gaps forming in the wrap, you need to make sure to keep a slight angle from the thread to the rod so that the thread will tend to pack against itself as it comes onto the rod. And remember, it is perfectly acceptable and even advisable to use your thumbnail after every few wraps to pack the thread back upon itself. This will result in a neater, smoother wrap. Once the thread has climbed onto the guide foot and begun to secure it, you can remove the tape holding the guide in place.

How far should you wrap up the guide foot? You will want to stop at that point where the thread begins to climb up onto the guide leg. But you do want to continue your wrap along the full length of the guide foot in order for the guide to be securely affixed to the rod. Of course, there is one more thing we must do before we end our wrap and that involves tying off our thread so the wrap will stay in place.

Try and estimate a distance that will be equal to about 5 or 6 winds of thread. When you are this far from what will be the end of your wrap, stop and put in your tie-off loop. You can use a piece of your wrapping thread or a piece of unwaxed dental floss for the loop, either will work fine. I suggest putting the loop in exactly 180 degrees opposite the guide. This will allow you to perform the tie off without the guide getting in your way. Slip the loop in under your last wrap with the looped end towards the guide ring. Continue the wrap until you are at the end of the level part of the guide foot, which if you have estimated properly, will give you about 5 or 6 thread wraps over the tie-off loop. Place your thumb directly on top of the junction of loop and oncoming thread and pin things down. Leaving your thumb in place, reach up with the other hand to the oncoming thread and cut it, leaving yourself about 3 or maybe 4 inches of thread. Wet the end of the the cut thread (to facilitate getting the free end through the loop) and pass it through the tie-off loop. Keep that thumb on the junction of the tie-off loop and thread end but ever so slightly release the pressure just enough so that with your other hand you can grasp the end of the tie-off loop and pull it back underneath your thumb and the wrap. Continue pulling until the free end of your wrapping thread is completely pulled through and out of the wrap. Good, you're almost done.

At this point you can relax a bit. The wrap is complete and isn't going anywhere. But you've got to cut the extra thread, the end you just pulled through the wrap, nice and neat so you don't end up with an ugly "nub" that your wrap finish will not cover. Do this: lie a single-edge razor blade flat across the wrap directly behind the free thread end. Now with the opposite hand bring the free end up and back across the razor blade, pulling backwards on the free end until it contacts the blade and cuts itself free. If you do this properly, the thread will stretch just enough so that when it is cut, it will snap back and pretty much disappear under the wrap. Use your thumbnail to smooth over the exit point and sit back and admire your handiwork.

Your first few wraps will be the hardest. Luckily, you will see great improvement as you go along, with each wrap getting better. At some point, and if you build enough rods, you will find that a simple thread wrap can be accomplished in less than a minute each, depending upon the area that needs to be covered.

Trim Wraps

Trim wraps are made exactly as the main guide wraps are made. Because they are usually narrow, you will find yourself putting in the tie-off loop almost immediately after you have started the wrap. You will want to begin any trim wraps against the edge of the standing guide wrap which will make things a bit easier as well. If you find that your first few trim-wrap attempts simply fly or fall apart upon completion, you may need to adjust thread tension slightly, use more wraps over your tie-off loop or beginning wrap, or a combination of all three. Don't get discouraged—it's just going to take some repetitive practice.

General Wrapping Tips

If you are a complete beginner, I strongly suggest making your first wraps on those guides nearest the butt. The blank is larger at that point and wraps made there are a bit easier than those farther out towards the tip. Working on the larger area of the rod first allows you to gain some experience before moving on to the smaller and more tedious area nearer the tip.

When wrapping guides, always start your wrap away from the guide, and wrap towards the guide. This allows the thread to climb up onto the guide foot and pack against itself. Wrapping the other direction will result in the thread "falling" off the guide foot near the edge and leaving an ugly gap. The only time you will wrap away from an object, is when making trim wraps which are begun against the standing guide wraps, and when making tip-top and grip trim wraps. These are started against the standing item and wrapped away from them.

Ferrule Reinforcement Wraps

On multi-piece rods, both tip-over-butt and spigot (plug)-type ferrules need to be reinforced near the female opening to prevent a split-out from starting at that point. The wrap tension should be a bit more snug than what you use on your guide wraps as you are trying to provide a bit of extra "hoop" strength in this area. (Do not wrap so tightly that you constrict the female opening which might prevent seating the ferrule completely.) On tip-over-butt ferrules the female ferrule should be wrapped, on spigot ferrules both the female ferrule and the area where the plug fits into what becomes the male ferrule need to be wrapped.

Make sure to wrap closely to the very edge of the ferrule opening, as this is the only place where a split-out can begin. It is this area closest to the ferrule opening that is most critical when making a ferrule reinforcement wrap. How long should the wrap be? In my opinion most builders make the reinforcement wrap much too long. I settled on a formula that sets the wrap length at twice the outside diameter of the ferrule at the female opening. In almost 20 years I have not had a single ferrule failure so I feel that this amount of reinforcement is quite sufficient.

You will find that it is easier to start your wrap at the edge of the ferrule opening and wrap away from it than to wrap towards it and try to perform your tie-off procedure at the edge. You will also benefit from inserting the butt section into the tip while you make the wrap. This allows you to have some support on both sides of the ferrule and thus have better control over the procedure.

One final thought that pertains to spigot/plug-type ferrules regards the built-in gap between the two sections when the ferrule is fully seated. This is not a defect, the exposed area is designed for future wear and allows the tip to seat further down on the spigot as time goes on. Do not grind or sand anything in an attempt to close this gap or you will wind up with a ferrule that will not join securely and will cast the tip off when casted.

Step 1: Rest the guide on a solid object such as a block of wood or vise. Use a standard fine-tooth metal file to taper the end of the foot. Remember to use long forward strokes with the file as this will remove the maximum amount of material in the least amount of time.

Step 2: This foot edge has been properly shaped and will be easy to wrap.

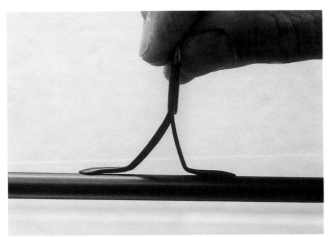

Step 3: Guides that do not sit perfectly flat on the blank can create dangerous stress points once wrapped and can cause a blank to fail over time. Bending and/or filing may be necessary to achieve a flat mating surface on the guide feet.

Step 4: A chainsaw file is an excellent device for fine-tuning the undersides of the guide feet. Lock the file in a vise and push the guide down and against the cutting teeth, moving it long strokes in the direction of cut only. Applying pressure in both directions will result in a quickly dulled file.

Step 5: Size your file to approximate the diameter of the blank where each respective guide will ultimately reside. Note the small amount of material removed from the guide underfoot in the photo. This guide will now sit perfectly flat on the blank surface.

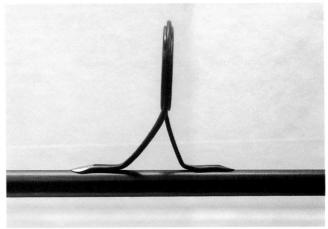

Step 6: This guide has been filed top and bottom, had its frame straightened and ground areas polished. It sits flat on the blank, will be easy to wrap and will never cause any damage to the blank.

Step 7: Affix two small strips of tape to the guide's feet and place the guide on the blank.

Step 8: Press the tape into contact with the blank. The tape does not need to be pressed together at the bottom, doing so will only make it harder to remove.

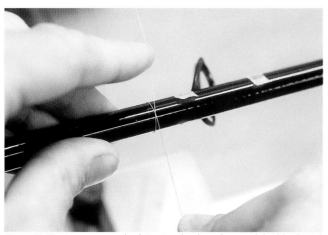

Step 9: Begin your wrap by bringing the thread around the blank and crossing it over the top of itself, forming an X. Some builders find it easier to begin this wrap freehand, others will make a one-revolution wrap of masking tape just away from the edge of the guide foot to act as a "stop" and to push the thread against. Do what is easiest for you.

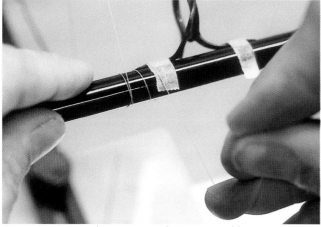

Step 10: Here is where most people get into trouble. You must wrap the tag end around the blank two or three times before proceeding with the wrap and hold the standing end as you wrap. Otherwise the X formed earlier will slip and revolve around the blank as you continue wrapping. Pay close attention to this photograph—it will save you some hair pulling.

Step 11: Use a finger to direct the thread along the desired path, making sure it continues to overwrap the standing end.

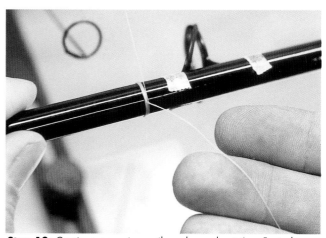

Step 12: Continue wrapping until you have about 4 or 5 winds over the standing thread.

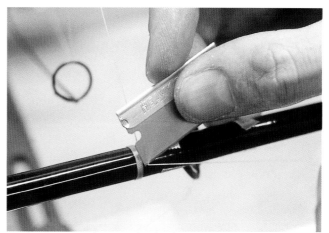

Step 13: Use a sharp single-edged razor blade to cut the standing end. It need not be flush with the wrap as you will wrap over it.

Step 14: Your thumbnail is your friend and should be used to keep the thread wrap neat and packed together. Adjust the angle of the oncoming thread if you are getting too many gaps.

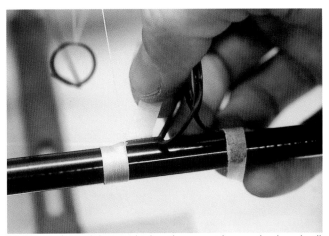

Step 15: If you did a good job with your guide prep the thread will climb up and onto the guide foot with little trouble. Nevertheless, you may still have to use your thumbnail to keep the threads together as you come around each time. Do not hesitate to "help" the thread climb onto the guide foot if it resists.

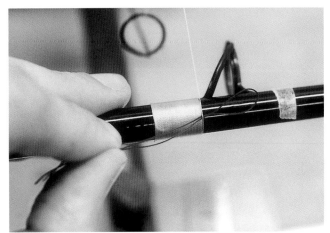

Step 16: As you approach the area where it appears you are about 5 or 6 revolutions from the point on the guide where the foot turns into a leg, insert a tie-off loop made from scrap D-size thread.

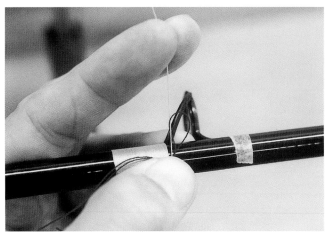

Step 17: Continue wrapping those next 5 or 6 revolutions and cut the oncoming thread. Study the photograph carefully and try to mimic the hand position at this point.

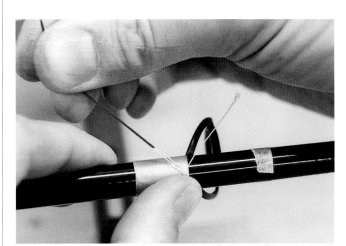

Step 18: Insert the cut end into and through the tie-off loop and pull the tie-off loop back under and through the wrap until the cut end is pulled completely through.

Step 19: Pull the cut end back so that you form a small opening in the wrap where the end came through.

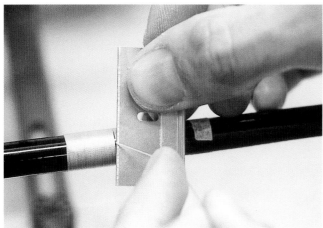

Step 20: Press a sharp razor blade against the free end and cleanly cut the excess thread off by bringing it back against the blade.

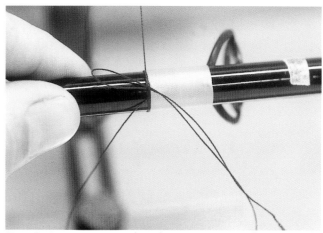

Step 1: A trim wrap is made in the same manner as the main guide wrap, except the tie-off loop must be put in almost immediately. Begin the wrap against the guide wrap and wrap away from it. Don't be surprised if your first few attempts fly apart. It takes practice.

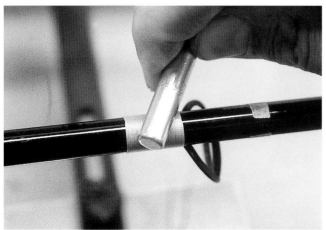

Step 21: Use a thumbnail or round object to close the gap and smooth the wrap.

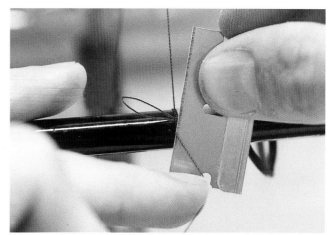

Step 2: After wrapping over the standing end just 2 or 3 winds, cut the standing end flush as possible with the remainder of the wrap.

Step 22: The finished wrap.

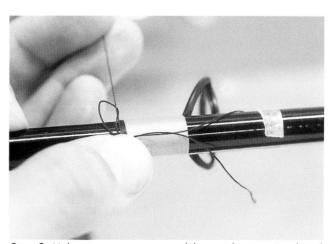

Step 3: Make one or more wraps and then cut the oncoming thread and insert it through the loop just as you did when making the previous guide wrap.

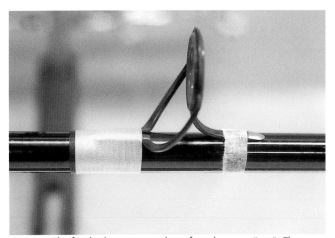

Step 4: The finished trim wrap, also referred to as a "tag". The more narrow you make it, the better it will look. Of course, the more narrow it is the more difficult it is to make! Practice makes perfect.

On single-foot guides it is often a good idea to make a "security" wrap which effectively locks the guide in place. To make one, just continue the wrap around and behind the guide leg as shown here.

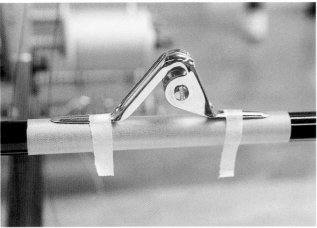

Larger guides used in heavy-duty applications are often wrapped on top of an "underwrap" of A size thread. Some people will coat the underwrap with an application of color preserver before making the overwrap on the guide. Consult the text for available options in this regard.

The finished wrap with security wrap as an integral part of the overall wrap.

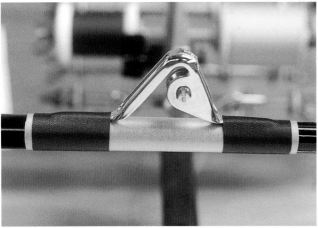

The overwrap of D-size thread is made and the wrap is complete.

Over the years I have become very accustomed to meeting a first-time rod builder who has just completed his or her first rod. Usually they will hand their new rod over for my inspection and then quickly make some sort of apology for the finish, whose appearance is obviously somewhat less than what they had hoped for. The finish on your thread wraps is not only a functional aspect of the rod, it is the final cosmetic touch that tells others something about the quality of the work that lies underneath. All too often, minor mistakes and incorrect application techniques mar what would otherwise have been a beautiful finished product.

Two-part epoxy rod finishes have revolutionized the finishing of thread windings. They are extremely durable, long wearing and somewhat flexible to boot. But for many first-time rod builders, epoxy finishes are also difficult to work with as they can be very temperamental. Luckily, with a basic understanding of how these finishes work and the best way to apply them, you can achieve very nice results the first time out.

Color Preserver

If you wrap-finish directly on the threads, they will turn dark, almost translucent. And, they will stay that way even after the wrap-finish has dried. Some rod builders prefer this dark, translucent look and there is nothing wrong with it. Others, however, prefer to have their threads remain bright and vibrant, just as they appear on the spool. For that reason acrylic color preservers have been developed which will penetrate and seal the wrapping threads so that the final finish cannot further penetrate and thus change the appearance of the thread.

If you wish to retain the color vibrancy of your thread you will want to use color preserver. Follow the manufacturer's thinning and application directions carefully. Make sure

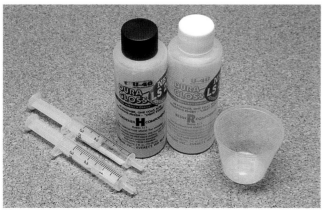

The most common type of rod wrap finish in use today is 2-part epoxy. There are some other alternatives available however.

that you apply enough so that the threads turn uniformly dark and then remove any excess with your brush. Some color preservers require a second application, although one full wet coat will usually suffice. Again consult the directions on the bottle and follow them closely. Wait 24 hours and then proceed with your wrap-finish.

At some point you will no doubt hear that color preserver creates a wrap which is inherently weak. It doesn't of course, but make no mistake that such wraps are not quite as strong as those where wrap-finish is applied directly to the threads. Still, wraps made with color preserver are more than strong enough to weather many, many years of hard use without failure. Consider the use of color preserver from a cosmetic standpoint only, as wrap strength is not the issue some make it out to be.

Types

Let me start by saying that of all the various epoxy finishes formulated, bottled or sold for this purpose, none are in any way bad or troublesome. I state this because all too often a rod builder will make a mistake in measuring or mixing a particular finish, experience problems and then blame that particular brand as if it was unsuitable for finishing thread wraps. Nothing could be further from the truth. All of the epoxy rod-building finishes of which I am aware will yield excellent results provided they are properly used. Ninety-nine times out of 100, when a problem occurs, it is the fault of the finisher, not the finish.

Most of the companies who market epoxy rod finish offer two viscosities; "lite" or regular "high-build". The names can be somewhat confusing as the "lite" formulas can be built up to a thick coating by applying several coats, and the "high-build" formulas can yield a thin finish by just applying a bit less and using a stiffer brush to remove any excess. I am not going to recommend one over the other, except to say that most beginners will get better results by applying finish conservatively and using, if necessary, multiple coats or applications to achieve the desired depth.

Apparatus

For starters, let me go ahead and mention that it is absolutely imperative that you get an exact 1 to 1 mix of resin and hardener. Failure to adhere to this ratio will result in a finish that simply will not harden, ever. The very best method for assuring a perfect 1 to 1 mix is the use of syringes. Not just any syringes mind you, but those sold by the same firms who also market and sell epoxy rod-wrap finish. These syringes will not contain any silicone release agents which can contaminate your epoxy and result in all sorts of peculiarities and problems. If you are planning to use syringes obtained from the local drug store, don't. Use those provided with your finish or obtain a pair from the manufacturer of your finish.

For a mixing container, you should select a small container, glass or metal are best, with smooth sides and bottom. A common shot glass makes a perfect mixing bowl. The smooth sides will not trap unmixed finish and it is easily wiped out and cleaned after use. For stirring, you should use a non-porous mixing stick, something along the lines of a metal spatula or the smooth handle from an old spoon or fork.

There are many brushes available for applying epoxy rod finish. I like the common ox hair artist/hobby brushes about a 1/4 to 1/2 inch in width that sell for a couple bucks apiece. They're soft enough to allow you to get enough finish on the wraps and can be cleaned and reused for several applications. Stay away from the cheap disposable brushes sold for applying flux or glue. They're too stiff for applying rod finish and will give you nothing but problems.

Finishing Environment

Epoxy finishes should be used in an area with some ventilation. Unlike other products, epoxy finishes are easily tolerated by most people, but breathing the vapors or allowing it to come into contact with bare skin is still not a good idea. A very, very few people are allergic to it and can have rather bad reactions. Give yourself a bit of breathing room and try not to get it on your hands or in your eyes.

Temperature and humidity can play a role in how fast, or slow, an epoxy finish gels and cures. Extremes in either direction may not preclude curing but will greatly affect the time it takes to do so. A simple rule of thumb is this, if you're comfortable, your finish will be too. If you're not, adjust the temperature or humidity to your own comfort zone. Within that zone, your finish will gel and cure as expected.

Pay particular attention to temperature. A 20°F. swing in either direction from about 70°F. can either double or half the cure time. If you find that your finish won't harden, and you applied it in a very cool, if not downright cold, area, move it into a warmer place and it should cure properly. Better yet, do your finishing in the proper environment to start with.

Measuring and Mixing

How careful you are in terms of measuring and mixing your finish will determine how well, or even if, your finish will set-up and cure properly. It is the minor mistakes made here that cause the vast majority of all rod-finishing problems.

Now that you have the proper device for measuring your resin and hardener (syringes), let's talk a bit about amounts. Often a rod builder will not wish to waste finish so he or she will only mix the absolute minimum required to do the job at hand. This is where many a problem begins.

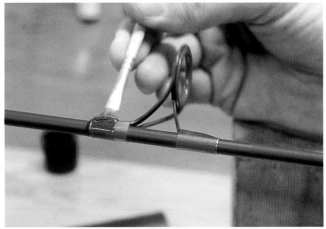

Load the brush with epoxy finish and hold it against the wrap while rotating the rod underneath it. Notice the wooden block in the background that my hand is resting on. This allows for a steady hand.

Long areas are best finished with lengthwise brush strokes. This helps you get a more uniform coating on the rod and also allows the finish to level better.

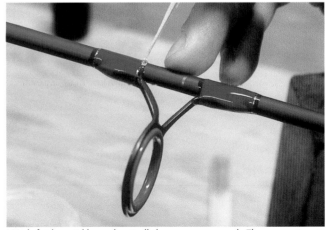

Work fairly quickly and get all the wraps covered. The epoxy is setting up as you work! After all the wraps are covered, go back and touch in any thin or "dry" areas. In the photo, I am putting a drop of epoxy into the tunnel formed between the guide foot, thread wrap, and blank. This will prevent water from entering and undermining the wrap at a later date.

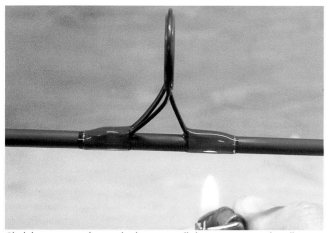

Slightly warming the applied epoxy will thin it momentarily, allowing bubbles to escape. Keep the flame a couple inches under the wrap and never allow the flame to touch the finish. Rotate the rod quickly as you do this—you only want to warm the finish, not cook it. Some epoxies do not respond well to this technique and some simply do not need the application of heat in order to release bubbles. Consult the instructions that came with your finish to determine the best methods to use with your particular brand.

Let's say your measuring skills are off just a little bit and your total 2cc mix is off on one of the two parts by 1/2cc. This adds up to a mix ratio that is off by a whopping 25%! But if you mix up a larger 6cc mixture and are off by that same 1/2cc on one of your two parts, now you're only off by about 8% from that ideal 1 to 1 mix ratio. My point is that many a finish job has been ruined by a rod builder's "thriftiness". Fill the syringes completely, normally this is 3ccs each, and just throw out what you don't use afterwards. Trust me, this will save you many a headache down the road.

Use your spatula to slowly, yet thoroughly, mix the finish you have discharged into your mixing container. Do not stir too quickly or you will introduce quite a few bubbles into the mix. At first, the finish will appear cloudy. As the two parts begin to thoroughly mix, it will start to turn clear. I recommend stirring for at least a full additional minute *after* the finish has become clear. Make sure to scrape the sides of the mixing container as you stir and blend both parts of the finish together.

You may work directly from your mixing container, although many rod builders prefer to pour their mixed finish out onto a piece of aluminum foil. This will extend the working time of the mix by a few minutes as well as allow a few of the inevitable bubbles introduced during mixing to escape.

Application

Realizing that the two-part epoxy rod finish is curing before his eyes, the average rod builder should develop a sense of urgency. Too many builders, however, will labor intensely over each guide, taking minutes to get each one just right, only to find that as they get halfway up the rod, the finish has begun to gel and is going on like cold syrup.

Don't waste time getting the finish on each guide perfect, yet. Apply it as nicely and evenly as you can and quickly move on to the next guide. You can return later and touch-up any dry areas with a drop of finish on a toothpick or the corner of your brush *after* you've gotten all the wraps decently covered. It should take well under a minute to apply finish to a guide wrap, including larger wraps like those found on the big saltwater sticks.

Remember that in most cases you can continue to work with your finish in some fashion for up to an hour after you've mixed it. But during that time, it is gelling more and more. This is why I suggest getting the wraps covered quickly, while the finish is still liquid and flowing. Trying to work finish onto a wrap and around guide feet after it has taken on the consistency of chewing gum is almost impossible. Once you've gotten everything covered you can relax and take your time attending to any small imperfections.

Attend to any dry areas by applying a spot of finish. If this is done within the first hour, such spot repairs will flow and level nicely. Remove any excess epoxy finish with your brush or wipe it off exposed blank areas with a rag moistened with alcohol. There will come a time, however, when you will have done all you can do for the time being, and can only watch your handiwork as it cures.

I would be remiss if I did not discuss the process of warming the finish slightly so that bubbles can escape. During the mixing and application of your finish, some amount of bubbles entered your finish. Some will escape on their own, but as the finish gels, some can become trapped in the finish. Using a small disposable lighter, hold the flame a couple of inches under each wrap while you rotate the rod. The warmth from the flame will temporarily thin the epoxy and allow the bubbles to escape to the surface. It is not necessary to apply a lot of heat to the finish, nor should you allow the flame to come into contact with the actual wrap or the finish. I have seen rod builders "flame" the finish with a propane torch, but this is not necessary. A moment's application of gentle heat is all that is required. Obviously, you should use any source of open flame carefully in order to reduce and/or eliminate any chance of injury. Some rod builders have successfully utilized hair dryers for this purpose and if you can keep airborne dust and debris from alighting on the wraps, this is a safer alternative.

Some rod builders place their rod in a turning device so that the finish will not sag or run while drying. This is an acceptable practice and if you choose to do this make sure the entire rod is level. Failure to level the rod will cause the finish to do some funky things. You can make your own finish rotator/dryer from some V-blocks and an old rotisserie motor, or buy a commercially manufactured unit from most any rod-building supply house.

However, it is not necessary to use any sort of rotation device in order to achieve a nice, level, smooth finish. Again, making sure your rod is resting perfectly level, point the guides straight up. In a few minutes the finish will start to sag to the bottom. At the first notice of this, spin the rod 180 degrees so the guides are pointing straight down. Turn the rod 180 degrees every few minutes to prevent finish sag. As the finish begins to gel, the time between rotations can increase. You will want to continue rotating the rod for about 2 hours or more, depending upon the brand finish you are using, as well as the temperature where you are working. To be safe, I have often recommended turning the rod up and down for three hours. That usually covers the time it takes for nearly all the popular finishes to gel sufficiently. This is a good time to have a book handy, or maybe a TV, so you can have something to do while you turn the rod every few minutes.

In the event that you decide to apply another application, you should wait until the next day before doing so. It is not necessary to sand or scuff the previous application, unless you have waited more than a day or two.

Finishing Alternatives

I have been telling you about epoxy finishes, almost assuming that you will have chosen that type of coating for your thread wraps. While it is true that epoxy rod finishes offer good protection, ease of use and beauty, I would be remiss if I did not mention another equally effective rod coating. For many years, single-part evaporated-type coatings such as varnish and shellac were used as thread coatings. Long-term durability was a problem and when tougher epoxy coatings came along most rod builders embraced then readily as a better alternative. During the time epoxy coatings were taking the rod-building hobby by storm, urethanes went almost unnoticed. Actually, certain urethanes are even tougher than epoxy and offer greater abrasion resistance and better long-term clarity than epoxy. So why haven't rod builders taken a look at the urethanes, you ask? For starters, many are simply unaware of urethane as a quality rod-wrap coating. Others have tried urethane but quickly grown tired of the multiple coats needed for adequate depth, particularly on heavier saltwater rods which might require as many as 5 to 10 coats! And I haven't even mentioned the fact that once a jar of urethane is opened, it begins to cure from the moist air introduced into the jar. Many a urethane user has cracked opened a jar of finish to use on a just-wrapped rod only to find that the urethane has completely solidified since its last use.

However, there is still a place for urethane as a thread coating. If you desire a thin, light coating for your fly rods and ultra-light spinning rods, or even a heavy, tough, abrasion-resistant, water-clear finish for your biggest saltwater surf and trolling rods, urethane may be the finish for you. The particular brand I recommend is manufactured by Trondak and is sold under the trade name U-40 Perma-Gloss. Earlier I mentioned that some types of urethane made excellent thread coatings. Perma-Gloss is one of those. Unlike some urethanes that yellow upon exposure to ultraviolet light, Perma-Gloss remains water-clear forever. It offers a hard, yet flexible coating that will best even epoxy rod finish on all fronts. Perhaps the only downside is the multiple coats that are required and the chance that it will solidify in the bottle before you get a second rod done. Still, it is a viable and even superior thread coating if you find that epoxy does not suit your tastes.

Whether you choose epoxy or urethane, modern thread-wrap coatings have improved tremendously over the past few decades and you and your new rod are the beneficiary of these advancements. If all goes well, you will have achieved a beautiful, glass-like finish over your thread wraps with either type. One that will protect as well as show off your work for years to come.

Chapter 9

Further Techniques

Most beginning rod builders are satisfied with buying a blank and pre-made components and assembling their first rod. But many of you will get the urge to expand your rod-building activities by making or altering some of the component parts that go into a custom rod. One of the first areas that such aspiring rod builders expand into is grips and handles. Even with all the pre-made units on the market, you may wish to create a special shape that seems more comfortable for you. You might desire a higher grade of cork than what is available in a pre-made grip. Maybe you want to add some distinctive decorative touch that sets your custom rod apart. Regardless of why you want to do it, making your own handles and grips is not only easy, but very satisfying.

Turning Cork Handles and Grips

By purchasing individual cork rings, gluing them up and turning them yourself, you can obtain any shape or size grip you wish. Because it is possible to buy individual cork rings in a higher grade or quality than what is used on most pre-made grips, you can also arrive at a grip that feels and looks better.

Before you buy your own individual rings, I want to mention that as the quality goes up (smoother surface, less imperfections) the price skyrockets! The best-quality cork rings sell for as much as a couple bucks each. And that's for rings which are only 1/2 inch in length! So using the very best cork on a grip that you intend to be say, 8 inches long, will cost you $16 just for the material. Dropping back one or two grades, to cork which is just as functional but perhaps not quite as pretty, can save you a bundle. Although I'm never one to talk a rod builder out of choosing and using the best, some builders go overboard on their cork selection. Once used, cork quickly becomes soiled and the cosmetic difference between the very best grade and one grade lower is quite negligible. I suggest buying the highest grade that will allow you to eliminate imperfections which are large enough to create discomfort in the hand. Beyond that, you just have to decide how much you wish to spend to have a prettier rod, and then only for awhile. There is no standard in naming cork grades among suppliers, so you may wish to buy a few rings in various grades from different vendors before deciding which grade and which dealer to go with.

Rings can be glued-up either directly on the blank or on a steel turning mandrel. There are two schools of thought here. One insists that it is easier and more secure to ream and fit individual rings to the blank and then turn the grip on the blank. The other school believes that mounting and turning the rings on a mandrel and then hand reaming to fit the completed grip to the blank is more convenient. There are pros and cons to each. If you choose to turn your grip on the blank, you will need a lathe that will handle the length of the

blank. If you make a mistake, you are also faced with having to cut the grip off the blank before you can start again. With a steel turning mandrel, a smaller lathe or even drill press can be employed. But, once complete, you must carefully ream out the grip to accurately fit the blank. I believe each method works equally well and have employed both at times. For most rod builders, turning the grip off the rod with a steel turning mandrel is more convenient, so we'll use that method for illustration this time out.

To start, you will need to acquire a steel mandrel for mounting the rings. These are available from some blank and components dealers or you can have a machine shop supply you with a length of drill rod. These are not expensive. Try to use the shortest mandrel that will accept the longest grip you plan on turning, plus the length needed for chucking in the lathe head and for support on the opposite end. If you have a lathe with a live center, have a machine shop bore a 60-degree conical center in one end to accept the live center. Most cork rings are supplied with a 1/4-inch bore, so a 1/4-inch mandrel is what you will want. Larger diameters are available and you can bore your rings to accommodate these larger mandrels which will greatly reduce your reaming time on the completed grip if you are mounting on a rod with a very large diameter butt area. But if you are careful and don't mind a few extra minutes spent hand reaming, the 1/4-inch set-up is the simplest way to go, and probably what you'll want for most fly and light freshwater rods.

Using a piece of paraffin wax, which is available at most hardware and even some grocery stores, rub the block of wax up, down and around the mandrel a few times. This will prevent the cork grip from permanently adhering to the mandrel once complete. Count out the number of rings you will need to complete your grip. Slide one ring down onto the mandrel. Now thoroughly coat one surface of the next ring with two-part slow-cure epoxy, or Rod Bond, and slide it down onto the mandrel until it seats onto the first ring. It is not necessary push them together tightly at this point. Proceed with the next ring and the next until you have mounted all the rings onto the mandrel. Now you must compress the grip assembly to fully seat the rings against each other and eliminate any voids or gaps. It is possible to accomplish this with several heavy rubber bands, or some type of vise arrangement, but the preferred method is with a simple tool known as a cork clamp. If you plan to make many grips, you should invest in, or make, one of these useful tools. Most dealers carry them for well under $20 or you can make your own with some small scraps of wood, some threaded rod and a few wing-nuts. (See the accompanying photos.)

There is no need to go overboard with your clamping pressure. Just make sure to compress the rings enough so that no voids or gaps exist between any of the rings. As you do this, quite a bit of excess epoxy will be squeezed out of the assembly. This is normal. Wipe off as much as you can with a paper towel and set the assembly aside to dry overnight.

After the epoxy has set, you can remove the clamp and chuck the mandrel into your turning apparatus. Turing cork is sort of a dirty business and cork dust and debris will quickly cover the area in and around your work area. To minimize the mess, you might try rigging a shop vac in such a way as to catch most of the dust, or do your turning outside where the cork dust won't matter. Either way, be sure to wear eye protection and even consider a dust mask to protect your lungs from having to deal with this fine dust. In order to get the shape you want, you might wish to work from a rough sketch you have made, or copy the grip on a favorite rod. In any event, work slowly and start turning with fairly coarse sandpaper. (If you are using a regular wood lathe and have standard wood-turning tools, I suggest first using a round or square-ended scraper to make the grip assembly concentric with the center and for removing any excess epoxy that was forced out of the grip.) Use something like 80 grit for roughing out the general shape you desire. Once you have gotten close to the desired size and shape, drop to 120 or 150 grit for final shaping. Once the general shape is nearly complete move to 220 and then to 320, followed by 400 for final polishing. If you fail to work through the various grades, in order, you will not achieve a velvety smooth surface on the grip. Keep in mind as well, that the finer grades of sandpaper will not remove large amounts of cork. That is why you must do the majority of your actual shaping with the coarser grades, such as 80 and 150 grit.

First-time grip turners are apt to make mistakes. Too much cork comes off in one area, not enough in another. The only fix for this is experience. I often recommend that novice grip turners purchase some low-grade, inexpensive cork and turn several "practice" grips before starting on a grip meant for a prized rod. As in many aspects of rod building, working slowly and carefully and checking your work often, will result in better results than quick, forced effort will.

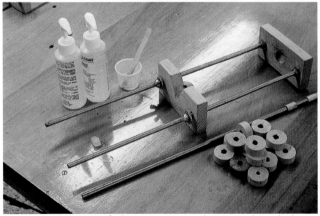

The required pieces to fashion your own cork grip. Cork, cork clamp, mandrel, parrafin wax and 2-part epoxy.

Step 1: Wipe the mandrel with the parrafin wax. This will prevent the epoxy used in gluing the cork rings from permanently affixing our grip to the mandrel.

Step 2: Mix the epoxy and coat one side of a cork ring with adhesive.

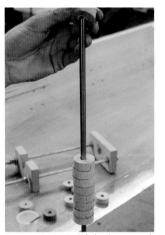 

Steps 3 & 4: Slide the ring down onto the mandrel, adhesive side up. Continue in this fashion until all the rings are in place. No adhesive is necessary on the surface of the last ring.

Step 5: The cork rings, glued and ready to be clamped.

Step 6: The assembly in the cork clamp. It should be left in the clamp for several hours.

Step 7: After the epoxy has cured, the grip assembly is placed in the appropriate turning device. Notice the shield in front of the chuck and the shop vac nozzle positioned to catch most of the dust and debris.

Step 8: A Stanley "SurForm" file/rasp is being used to remove the epoxy "skin" that formed during the gluing of the cork rings.

Step 9: A wood scraper is used to make sure the cork stick is concentric with the mandrel. Don't overdo this—just make sure the scraper is taking material from all sides.

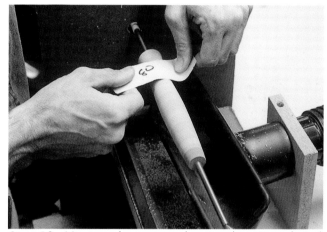

Step 10: 80-grit sandpaper is used to "rough out" our desired shape. Narrow strips work best if you need to shape a grip with subtle indentations such as this half wells fly-rod grip. Once the desired shape is attained, move through finer and finer grades of sandpaper, being careful not to skip any grades. By the time you reach 320-grade paper, you will have a nice smooth finish.

Step 11: A final sanding with 400 silicon carbide paper will give you a grip with a velvety smooth finish, if you so desire.

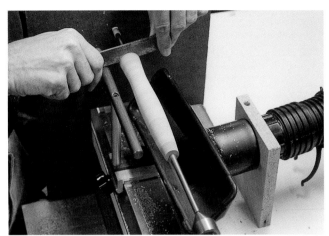

Step 12: The ends of the grip are squared with a rasp and a light sanding with 320 paper is performed to slightly round over the edges.

Step 13: Our finished grip, ready to "pop" off the mandrel and mount to the rod.

Decorative Butt Wraps

Many rod builders enjoy embellishing their custom rod with some unique feature in an effort to add a measure of distinction to their new creation. Most often this comes in the form of some type of decorative butt wrap such as the classic "diamond wrap". Be aware that decorative thread wrapping is such an extensive and fascinating endeavor that an entire book, and a large one at that, could be written exclusively on that subject in order to even begin to thoroughly cover such wrapping techniques. Still, we'll take a moment here and walk you through the steps of making a simple diamond wrap. Once mastered, you can use the technique to expand into other, more intricate wraps which you may design yourself or pick up from other sources.

The basic diamond is an open wrap, meaning that the background, or underlying area will show between each diamond. If you wish the blank to show between each diamond, do not make an underwrap for the diamond wrap. If you want to add a bit more color, or some degree of greater contrast, underwrap the area under which the diamonds will sit with thread in the color of your choice.

In order to align our diamonds, which will create a much neater, more precise and a better-looking wrap, use a piece of white NCP thread to make the reference marks for the point where the thread will cross to form each diamond. Use a length of thread that is slightly longer than twice your intended wrap length. (Doubling the thread makes this marking procedure go much more quickly.) Use a soft lead pencil to make these marks as ink will "spread" and make the marks less than precise.

How far apart you make these marks will determine the general shape of your diamonds. If the distance between centers is roughly the same as the diameter of the blank at that point, the diamonds will be about square. If the distance is less than the diameter of the blank, the diamonds will be somewhat compressed. Make the distance greater, and the diamonds will be elongated. If you are just starting out, I'd suggest spacing the marks about 1/2 of whatever your blank diameter might be at the area where the wrap will be constructed. This will give you a diamond that is nearly square. For example, if you are working on a diameter of about 1 inch, make your marks on the thread at every 1/2-inch interval. You may find it easier to work with millimeters on very small diameter blanks.

Cut the thread into two equal lengths and tape the end of one length on the 0-degree axis, squarely against the foregrip. Stretch the thread out and tape the other end down on the blank. Now spin the rod and tape the other length of thread to the blank in the same fashion but on the 180-degree axis. Now wrap some masking tape around the blank, at both ends of the alignment threads, for a few turns before doubling the tape back over itself and winding a wrap or two that way and affixing it to itself. By doing this you form a "tacky" surface that will allow you to stick down the wrapping threads.

Starting with the first thread, the one that will form the very center of the diamond, wrap around the blank at the foregrip a time or two and then spiral it up the blank, crossing the alignment threads at every other alignment mark. When you reach the top of your wrap area, tack the thread down on the upturned masking tape. Now take another length of thread and wrap it in the same fashion around the blank, starting at the foregrip but in the opposite manner so that it will cross the first thread at each alignment mark. When you reach the top of the wrap area tack it down. What you have just done is complete the centers of the diamonds. Each crossing point of those two threads will form the center of each diamond. If you wish the diamond centers to be wider than one thread, and it is likely that you will, continue wrapping threads in the same sequence as before until you reach the width you prefer. Some builders will wrap more than one thread at a time so as to accomplish the same task in less time. If you can do it, fine. Treat the width of multiple threads as a single band and the overall effect will be the same, but will culminate much more quickly.

Step 1: A piece of white NCP thread is marked for use as an alignment and center measurement "tool".

Step 2: The marked thread is taped into position at the 0- and 180-degree axis' of the blank. Make sure the alignment marks on the thread at each axis line up with each other.

Step 3: Masking tape is wound around the blank at each end of the alignment thread and then doubled back onto itself for one wind creating a sticky surface for us to "lock" our threads onto. This process may need to be repeated once the first layer of tape becomes crowded with thread.

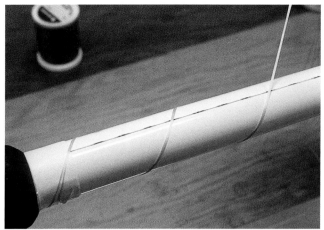

Step 4: Our first thread is wound up the rod after being "tacked" down onto the tape. In this photo, we are using every fourth mark on the tape as a crossing point. Your wrap can be elongated or compressed depending upon how far apart you make your crossing point. Study the text for more information on wrap geometry. Notice that here we are wrapping 4 threads at one time. If you can do so, wrapping more threads will be a timesaver, but for most beginners its best to wrap one at a time.

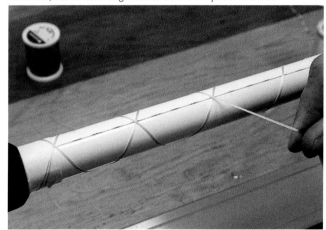

Step 5: The same procedure is being performed in this photo except that we are wrapping in the opposite direction now, forming crosses where the two thread wraps intersect. This is the basis for all decorative wraps.

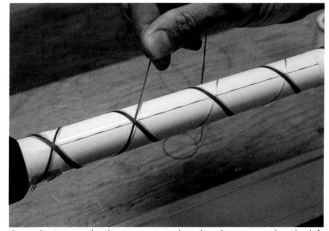

Step 6: A second color is now introduced and is wrapped to the left of the first threads that were wrapped. Notice that the threads coming toward you have already been wrapped and now the ones going away from you are being wrapped.

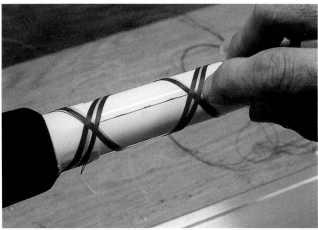

Step 7: Now the second color thread/s are wrapped to the right of the original color, both coming towards and going away from you. This action of wrapping on both sides of the wrap forms the basic diamond. If we wrapped additional threads only to the left, or only to the right, we could have what is known as a chevron. For a diamond, remember that whatever you do to one side of the wrap, you must do to the other. Make use of your thumbnail to keep the wrap packed together.

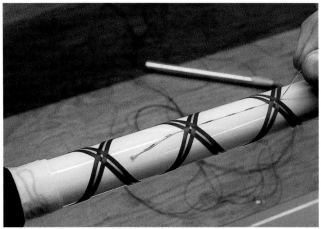

Step 8: Almost forgot the alignment thread! Not really. At this point the wrap is pretty much set and the NCP alignment thread can be cut at the ends and pulled out from under the wrap.

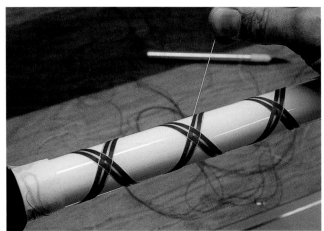

Step 9: The wrap is continued with a wrap of the original color, again working to both the left and the right of the wrap.

Step 10: The finished wrap, almost. Wrapping of the pattern is complete with the addition of a few wraps of the second color.

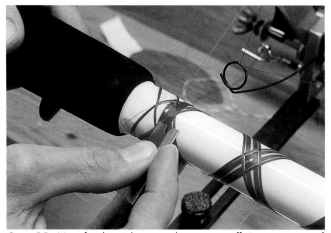

Step 11: Now for the tricky part—the wrap tie-off. Begin a wrap of thread on top of the diamond wrap just as you would if wrapping a guide. After four or five snug revolutions you can begin cutting the mess at the end of the wrap.

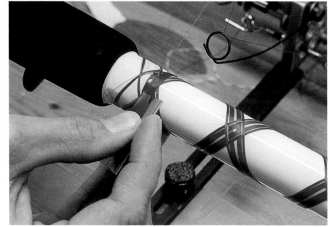

Step 12: BE CAREFUL! At this point it is very easy to cut the wrong thread or disturb the standing wrap. Work slowly and cut a few threads upon each revolution.

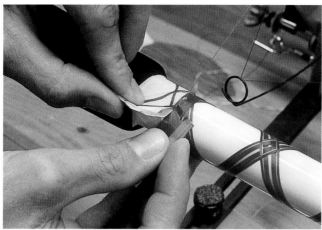

Step 13: As you continue to cut the threads, you will also have to cut through an occasional layer of tape. None of this is particularly hard, but care must be exercised as you do not want to inadvertently cut the oncoming thread ar any of the threads in the pattern which are exposed.

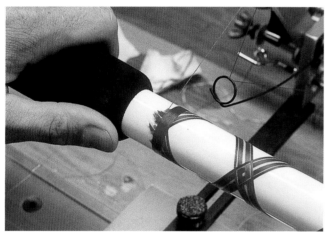

Step 14: Once the remainder of the threads and tape have been cut and removed you can continue with the tie-off wrap. Continue wrapping over the cut threads and when you reach the grip, continue the wrap back on top of itself and back towards where you started.

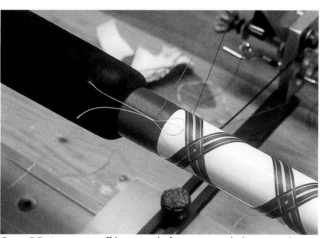

Step 15: Insert a tie-off loop just before you reach the original starting point and finish the wrap as usual.

Step 16: Viola! You have made your first diamond wrap! Well almost, you've still go to perform the tie-off on the upper end. Perform it exactly as you did this first one.

Just a sample of the kind of wraps you can make with the basics shown here.

As you wind the threads/bands, go back and use your thumbnail to push the thread junctions into alignment with the alignment marks. This will keep your wrap straight and centered. After you have wound a few threads or bands of thread, and aligned the centers properly, cut each end of the alignment thread near the extreme ends and pull each one out from under the diamonds. It has served its purpose and is no longer needed. If you wait too long to do this, it will be very difficult to remove it from under the diamonds.

In order to create the diamond, you will now wrap additional threads, or bands of thread on either side of the first two threads/bands. Remember to perform each task equally on either side and on each center thread/band so that your diamond will be concentric. (Adding more to one side or the other is the basis for more intricate designs which you may wish to learn later.) Develop a pattern so that you can remember where you are in the wrap. For instance, after forming your centers, wrap the next two threads/bands to the right of those already on the rod, then the next two to the left. What you do to one side, you must do to the other.

After a fashion, and once you have employed all the colors you wish, it will be time to tie-off the wrap. This is done in the same manner as when you tied-off your guide wraps. At the butt end, begin your tie-off wrap away from the foregrip and wrap towards it. At the opposite end, start your tie-off wrap away from the tip and wraps towards that end. After a few winds to lock in the threads forming the diamonds, begin to cut a few of the protruding threads from the diamond wrap after each wind. The idea is to completely cover the threads used to create the diamonds with these two tie-off wraps. As you near the ends of the wrap, carefully peel off the tape wraps you made when starting the wrap.

You may encounter your greatest difficulty at this point. Trying to cut the protruding diamond threads, wrap the tie-off and peel the darn masking tape off the rod all at the same time may be frustrating. Fortunately, a bit of patience will usually get you through and the experience gained after making a few of these decorative wraps will allow you to perform the tasks easily and quickly.

Complete the tie-off wraps in the same manner as you did your guide wraps, putting in a tie-off loop a few turns before you are finished with the wraps, and completing the wrap exactly as you did on each guide.

Finishing the diamond wrap is just like finishing a guide wrap, only it takes a bit more finish! If you used color preserver on the guide wraps, you will likely want to use it on the diamond wrap as well. Keep in mind that with any decorative wrap you have many threads on top of others. If you do not use color preserver and have made the wrap with regular nylon thread, quite of bit of bleed-through will occur. If however, you have used NCP thread to make the wrap, this will not be a problem. Most builders use the same thread for making both guide wraps and decorative butt wraps in order to provide consistency in appearance on the rod. Plan ahead and there will be no surprises later!

It is quite likely that you will need at least two coats of epoxy wrap-finish to cover your diamond wrap. If you used a urethane finish, it make take several more. With epoxy you will wish to wait overnight before applying the second coat, with urethane you may recoat in just a few hours. In either case, do not wait more than about 48 hours to apply a second application or the two may not bond/adhere to each other well. If in doubt as to what the particular application "window" for your finish is, contact the manufacturer and they will be happy to provide the information.

Care Of Your New Rod

Failure to properly store and transport rods often causes damage or breakage. If possible, transport rods in sturdy rod cases or tubes. Cloth bags also help prevent surface damage, but always make sure both the rod and bag are completely dry before storing a rod for any length of time. Multi-piece rods should always be disjointed before storage. In fact, it is a good idea to disassemble them at the end of each fishing day to prevent sticking as well as proper reseating before each day's fishing, which will keep you from throwing the tip off when casting.

I like to coat my new rods with an application of "lemon" furniture wax/polish in a spray. Something that contains some wax (not all do) is best. This makes it much easier to clean dirt, slime, scales, etc., off the rod after a fishing trip. Never use anything such as WD-40 on your rod. Some of these products contain solvents which will damage your thread-wrap coating. Instead, rinse or wash with clean, cool water and dry thoroughly. If your rods see quite a bit of use, you may wish to apply the furniture wax more than once a season.

EVA and cork grips can be cleaned by various methods. SOS pads, simple terry cloth hand towels and mild soap, or in dire cases, a Scotch Brite pad along with 409 or Fantastik will restore them to near-new condition.

Once you have the skills for wrapping guide rings, you might as well use it. Keep a check on your guides and tops for possible grooves (not very likely with good ceramic rings) or cracks which can occur from hard knocks. Replace any at the earliest possible time, or suffer the consequences of losing that fish of a lifetime. Cracked guide rings are murder on fishing line! Likewise, if you are using roller guides on heavy saltwater gear, make sure they turn freely. At least once each season you should remove the pins and screws and give them a thorough cleaning followed by lubricating with light grease. A locked roller will destroy your line in short order.

Finally a word is in order concerning the ferrules on multi-piece rods. Keep ferrule surfaces clean of sand, grit or grime. Do not apply any sort of lubricant or coating to them. They are made to perform best with a dry fit. (There is one product I will recommend however, it is called U-40 Ferrule Lube and will actually improve ferrule fit and durability.) Tip-over-butt and spigot (plug) ferrules should be joined by misaligning the guides, tip and butt, by about 90 degrees and then lightly seating the two sections. Now firmly twist the tip and butt sections into alignment while applying a bit of pressure against each. This will "lock" them into place and prevent any loosening during fishing. It is still a good idea to occasionally check the alignment and the tightness of the sections several times each day. Modern ferrules are extremely strong and durable provided they are kept tight and locked in place. To disassemble, simply untwist and pull apart.

It is recommended that multi-piece rods be disassembled at the end of each fishing day. In the rare event that a ferrule sticks and you cannot disassemble it, try putting it in front of an air conditioner and see if the contraction generated by the cold air will help the joint come loose. It may also help to use some sort of no-slip mat, such as often used in the kitchen for unscrewing the caps of food jars, to help you untwist a stuck ferrule. As a last resort, return the blank/rod to the manufacturer for disassembly. Relying on sheer, brute force is more likely to damage the rod than not.

Conclusion

As I wrote this book, I could not help but think of all the things I did not include. Putting down everything I have learned, witnessed or experienced in my 20-plus years of rod building would require many pages. While the information contained within should allow almost anyone to achieve good results on even a first rod, I am sure many questions will arise as you proceed with the process of building a rod. For that reason I am going to leave you with my mailing address and will attempt to provide answers to your questions as time permits. I am also going to list the address for the Custom Rod Builders Guild, an organization devoted to promoting custom rod building and the sharing of knowledge and techniques among builders. You may also find it helpful to subscribe to *RodMaker Magazine*. I must admit to some prejudice in this area as I am currently the editor. Still, the techniques and feature articles in each issue can help you move beyond the basics presented in this book and into the realm of the world-class rod builder, step by step, little by little.

As I stated at the outset, rod building can be addicting, you may find yourself embarking on a lifelong passion. With that in mind, I am already considering a follow-up book to this one, something that will cover more advanced techniques for those wishing to move beyond basic rod building into the world of truly custom-crafted fishing tools. Stay tuned.

Tom Kirkman
P.O. Box 1322
High Point, NC 27261

The Custom Rod Builder's Guild
PO Box 218121
Nashville, TN 37221-8121

RodMaker Magazine
PO Box 1322
High Point, NC 27261

OTHER HELPFUL BOOKS

ROD CRAFTING
by Jeffrey L. Hatton

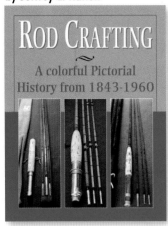

This unique, one-of-a-kind book is a must for anyone interested in the history of our great sport and collectors of antique fishing tackle. It takes a look at the history of fishing rods from the early 1800s to the 1970s, through text and hundreds of color photographs. With access to five private and extensive collections, Hatton covers the first three ages of rod-making: The smith age, up to 1870; the expansion era, 1870-1900; and the classic era, 1900-1970s. Forty-nine beautiful rods are featured, each with a description, history, notable features, and much more. Be warned: once you get into this book, you may look up to discover that several hours have gone by. 8 1/2 x 11 inches, 305 pages.

SB: $45.00   **ISBN: 1-57188-356-8**
                  UPC: 0-81127-00190-3
HB: $65.00   **ISBN: 1-57188-357-6**
                  UPC: 0-81127-00191-0

HANDCRAFTING A GRAPHITE FLY ROD
by L.A. Garcia

This book features 80 full-color step-by-step photographs and accompanying text for hand-crafting your own quality fly rod. Professional rod builder Garcia meticulously shows you exactly how to do it from selecting the blank to completing the wraps for a truly professional-looking rod. Large format for easy use. 8 1/2 x 11 inches, 48 pages.

SB: $15.95   **ISBN: 1-878175-58-0**
                  UPC: 0-66066-00146-7

CONSTRUCTING CANE RODS: SECRETS OF THE BAMBOO FLY ROD
by Ray Gould

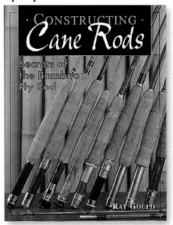

All-color book by master rod builder, Ray Gould. Includes: the history of cane, the creation of the machines and tools necessary to create your own rods, precise taper formulas, detailed schematic drawings with precise angles, step-by-step construction, finishing steps, formulas, repairs, historic cane manufacturers and model names, address and phone sources for all materials. Full color, 8 1/2 x 11 inches, 88 pages.

SB: $25.00   **ISBN: 1-57188-359-2**
                  UPC: 0-81127-00193-4

CANE RODS: TIPS & TAPERS
by Ray Gould

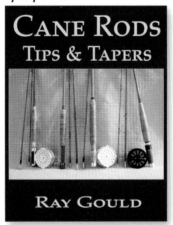

This book is intended as an aid for those who wish to pursue the art of cane-rod making or repairing. The reader will find a wealth of information regarding the methods, devices, and techniques that can only be learned by testing, trial and error. Many tips are given to guide the rod-maker in how to accomplish a particular and/or unusually difficult task. While a number of books and references are available for the basics of rod building, this book focuses on specific information and problem solving. The tips include: heat treating and moisture control; color toning; how to use and build equipment; ferrules; grips; rod wrapping; finishing and gluing; tapers; and more. Of special interest is an often sought after collection of nearly 300 rod tapers by many famous rod builders.

SB: $25.00   **ISBN: 1-57188-308-8**
                  UPC: 0-81127-00142-2

ASK FOR THESE BOOKS AT YOUR LOCAL FLY OR TACKLE SHOP.
IF UNAVAILABLE CALL OR FAX YOUR ORDER. ON THE WEB GO TO AMATOBOOKS.COM.
Frank Amato Publications, Inc. • P.O. Box 82112 • Portland, Oregon 97282
Toll Free 1-800-541-9498 (9-5 Pacific Time) • Fax (503) 653-2766